The Wicked Wit of Oscar Wilde

If, with the literate, I am
Impelled to try an epigram,
I never seek to take the credit;
We all assume that Oscar said it.

Dorothy Parker

The Wicked Wit of Oscar Wilde

Centenary Edition

Compiled by Maria Leach

Michael O'Mara Books Limited

This edition first published in Great Britain in 2000 by
Michael O'Mara Books Limited
9 Lion Yard
Tremadoc Road
London SW4 7NQ

Formerly published as *The Importance of Being A Wit*
in 1997 by Michael O'Mara Books Limited

A CIP catalogue record for this book is available from the British Library

ISBN 1-85479-807-3

3 5 7 9 10 8 6 4 2

Designed by Mick Keates
Typeset by Concise Artisans

Printed and bound in Finland by WS Bookwell, Juva

Contents

Publisher's Foreword

The year 2000 marks the centenary of the death of one of the most extraordinary figures in English letters – the Irish writer, socialite and, supremely, wit, Oscar Wilde. It is salutary to reflect, however, that a hundred years ago it seemed that his chances of immortality had been crushed for all time.

The instrument of the catastrophe that engulfed Oscar Wilde was innocuous enough in itself: a simple visiting card. On it, however, had been scrawled, 'To Oscar Wilde posing Somdomite [*sic*]'. The author of this charmless piece of goading was an irascible nobleman, John Sholto Douglas, eighth Marquess of Queensberry. In sending the card to Wilde at his club he hoped to spur the writer, then enjoying the very height of his fame and success, into making some foolish action or statement.

The Marquess's motive was clear enough: he wished to put an end to the relationship between his younger son, Lord Alfred Douglas, and Wilde, sixteen years the young man's senior. The friendship meant everything to Wilde, who showered 'Bosie' Douglas with presents, money, letters, advice; to Bosie's father, however, it reeked of unnatural vice and corruption of innocence. What had further infuriated Queensberry was that his efforts to halt the relationship had been met, as often as not, with some devastating sally of Wilde's, so that to the dishonour, as he saw it, of Bosie's unsuitable friendship was added the humiliation of being made the butt of the writer's wit.

The delivery of the visiting card was a public insult, and one that Wilde could scarcely ignore. He had received Queensberry's message on 18 April 1895, only four days after the triumphant opening night of *The Importance of Being Earnest*, and nothing must be allowed to sully the play's success. At Bosie's urging, he at once brought an action for criminal libel against the Marquess and, sensing a scandal, London society licked its lips. It was not to be disappointed, for Wilde's case collapsed under the weight of the evidence against him. Queensberry was exonerated, and Wilde's friends urged him to flee abroad to escape criminal prosecution. Unable to comprehend that his entire world had disintegrated, he refused, and in due course was himself arrested and charged with homosexual offences.

Wilde's flamboyant and unconventional lifestyle and, above all, his success, had earned him as many enemies as they had made him friends. Late-Victorian England was scandalized, and the playwright now found himself hurled down from the pinnacle he had occupied as one of society's darlings. Despite the evidence against him, however, when his case came to court on 26 April he defended himself with such brilliance that the jury were unable to reach a verdict.

A retrial was ordered, and this time the Establishment conquered; adjudged guilty, on 25 May 1895 Oscar Wilde was sentenced to two years at hard labour. It was barely three and a half months since his triumph at the opening of *The Importance of Being Earnest*.

On the night of his release in May 1897, Oscar Wilde sailed for France. By now bankrupt, divorced and cut off from his children for ever, he was never to set foot in England again. Taking the name Sebastian Melmoth, he hoped to remake his career as a writer; in the event, however, his sole work from this period was *The Ballad of Reading Gaol*, written in France and published in England anonymously in 1898. In exile, though occasionally visited by such loyal friends as Robert Ross and Max Beerbohm, and even by Bosie, his last years saw a sad decline into loneliness, self-disgust and failing health. Wilde died in Paris, from cerebral meningitis brought on by an ear infection, on 30 November 1900, destitute, embittered, broken and alone. He was forty-six years old.

Few writers have fallen so far, so swiftly. After his trial, Wilde's plays ceased to be performed, and his works fell out of print. Crushed beneath the full weight of late-Victorian piety, vilified as the most degraded example of *fin-de-siècle* decadence, he might easily have passed into near-obscurity as a literary curiosity. Yet before long it became clear that not just the theatre, but the entire literary and fashionable worlds, were a great deal poorer without him. Gradually his plays began to be restaged, his stories and other works to be reprinted; gradually, too, people began to recall his manner and, above all, his dazzling wit. A hundred years after his death, Wilde continues to gain new admirers in every corner of the world: no playwright except Shakespeare is as widely quoted, and few wits are as often or as happily recalled.

Accepting a glass of champagne shortly before his death, Wilde remarked to a friend, 'It would really be more than the English could stand if another century began and I were still alive.' At the dawn of yet another century – indeed, a new millennium – he remains an elemental figure in English literature. If that is surprising, given that the body of his work is relatively small and largely satirical, it is due perhaps to the measure of the man. For if Oscar Wilde was a wit without master, he was also much more than that, not least because, behind the aesthete's façade and the superbly crafted witticisms, he concealed great warmth of character and generosity of spirit, an insouciant gallantry in adversity, and a profound understanding of human life and human vanities. As a preface to this, the Centenary Edition of his collected sayings, the last word must belong to Wilde himself:

'We are all in the gutter, but some of us are looking at the stars.'

Age Before Beauty

Thirty-five is a very attractive age. London society is full of women of the very highest birth who have, of their own free choice, remained thirty-five for years. Lady Dumbleton is an instance in point. To my own knowledge she has been thirty-five ever since she arrived at the age of forty, which was many years ago now.

THE IMPORTANCE OF BEING EARNEST

The old believe everything: the middle-aged suspect everything: the young know everything.

PHRASES AND PHILOSOPHIES FOR THE USE OF THE YOUNG

Lord Illingworth: The soul is born old but grows young. That is the comedy of life.

Mrs. Allonby: And the body is born young and grows old. That is life's tragedy.

A WOMAN OF NO IMPORTANCE

I delight in men over seventy. They always offer one the devotion of a lifetime.

A WOMAN OF NO IMPORTANCE

. . . Lady Ruxton, an overdressed woman of forty-seven, with a hooked nose, who was always trying to get herself compromised, but was so peculiarly plain that to her great disappointment no one would ever believe anything against her.

THE PICTURE OF DORIAN GRAY

Beauty is the wonder of wonders. It is only the shallow people who do not judge by appearances.

THE PICTURE OF DORIAN GRAY

. . . A perfect saint amongst women, but so dreadfully dowdy that she reminded me of a badly bound hymn-book.

THE PICTURE OF DORIAN GRAY

Never trust a woman who wears mauve, whatever her age may be, or a woman over thirty-five who is fond of pink ribbons. It always means that they have a history.

THE PICTURE OF DORIAN GRAY

You're young and wouldn't be ill-favoured either, had God or thy mother given thee another face.

Vera, or The Nihilists

She has exquisite feet and hands, is always *bien chaussée et bien gantée*, and can talk brilliantly upon any subject, provided that she knows nothing about it.

The American Invasion

One can always tell from a woman's bonnet whether she has got a memory or not.

A Woman of No Importance

Lord Illingworth: I was very young at the time. We men know life too early.

Mrs. Arbuthnot: And we women know life too late. That is the difference between men and women.

A Woman of No Importance

To get back my youth I would do anything in the world, except take exercise, get up early, or be respectable.

The Picture of Dorian Gray

To Lord Arthur it came early in life – before his nature had been spoiled by the calculating cynicism of middle-age...

Lord Arthur Savile's Crime

Hesitation of any kind is a sign of mental decay in the young, of physical weakness in the old.

THE IMPORTANCE OF BEING EARNEST

What a pity that in life we only get our lessons when they are of no use to us!

LADY WINDERMERE'S FAN

No woman should ever be quite accurate about her age. It looks so calculating...

THE IMPORTANCE OF BEING EARNEST

There is nothing like youth. The middle-aged are mortgaged to Life. The old are in life's lumber-room.

A WOMAN OF NO IMPORTANCE

No life is spoiled but one whose growth is arrested.

THE PICTURE OF DORIAN GRAY

The youth of the present day are quite monstrous. They have absolutely no respect for dyed hair.

LADY WINDERMERE'S FAN

. . . A dowdy girl, with one of those characteristic British faces, that, once seen are never remembered.

THE PICTURE OF DORIAN GRAY

I never saw anybody take so long to dress, and with such little result.

THE IMPORTANCE OF BEING EARNEST

Thy body is hideous. It is like the body of a leper. It is like a plastered wall where vipers have crawled.

SALOMÉ

She was a curious woman, whose dresses always looked as if they had been designed in a rage and put on in a tempest.

THE PICTURE OF DORIAN GRAY

A really well-made buttonhole is the only link between Art and Nature.

PHRASES AND PHILOSOPHIES FOR THE USE OF THE YOUNG

She is still *décolletée* . . . and when she is in a very smart gown she looks like an *edition de luxe* of a bad French novel.

THE PICTURE OF DORIAN GRAY

A woman whose size in gloves is seven and three-quarters never knows much about anything.

An Ideal Husband

Nothing ages like happiness.

An Ideal Husband

As soon as people are old enough to know better, they don't know anything at all.

Lady Windermere's Fan

The only people to whose opinions I listen now with any respect are people much younger than myself.

The Picture of Dorian Gray

Fashion is what one wears oneself. What is unfashionable is what other people wear.

An Ideal Husband

Only the great masters of style ever succeed in being obscure.

Phrases and Philosophies for the Use of the Young

The two weak points in our age are its want of principle and its want of profile.

The Importance of Being Earnest

How can you see anything in a girl with coarse hands?

VERA, OR THE NIHILISTS

My experience is that as soon as people are old enough to know better, they don't know anything at all.

LADY WINDERMERE'S FAN

In America, the young are always ready to give to those who are older than themselves the full benefits of their inexperience.

THE AMERICAN INVASION

One should never trust a woman who tells one her real age. A woman who would tell one that, would tell one anything.

A WOMAN OF NO IMPORTANCE

The secret of life is never to have an emotion that is unbecoming.

A WOMAN OF NO IMPORTANCE

All beautiful things belong to the same age.

PEN, PENCIL AND POISON

I find it harder and harder every day to live up to my blue china.

[WHILE UP AT OXFORD, C. 1877]

There is nothing to my mind more coarse in conception and more vulgar in execution than modern jewellery.

HOUSE DECORATION

THE LAST ROMANCE

Men always want to be a woman's first love. That is their clumsy vanity. We women have a more subtle instinct about things. What we like is to be a man's last romance.

A Woman of No Importance

There's nothing in the world like the devotion of a married woman. It's a thing no married man knows anything about.

Lady Windermere's Fan

As for marriage, it is one of their most popular institutions. The American man marries early, and the American woman marries often; and they get on extremely well together.

The American Man

The worst of having a romance of any kind is that it leaves one so unromantic.

THE PICTURE OF DORIAN GRAY

Who on earth writes to him on pink paper? How silly to write on pink paper! It looks like the beginning of a middle-class romance. Romance should never begin with sentiment. It should begin with science and end with a settlement.

AN IDEAL HUSBAND

The only difference between a caprice and a life-long passion is that the caprice lasts a little longer.

THE PICTURE OF DORIAN GRAY

When one is in love one begins by deceiving oneself. And one ends by deceiving others. That is what the world calls a romance.

A WOMAN OF NO IMPORTANCE

Romance is the privilege of the rich, not the profession of the unemployed.

THE MODEL MILLIONAIRE

I am disgraced; he is not. That is all. It is the usual history of a man and a woman as it usually happens, as it always happens. And the ending is the ordinary ending. The woman suffers. The man goes free.

A WOMAN OF NO IMPORTANCE

The amount of women in London who flirt with their own husbands is perfectly scandalous. It looks so bad. It is simply washing one's clean linen in public.

THE IMPORTANCE OF BEING EARNEST

Lord Illingworth: Women have become too brilliant. Nothing spoils a romance so much as a sense of humour in the woman.

Mrs. Allonby: Or the want of it in the man.

A WOMAN OF NO IMPORTANCE

I assure you women of that kind are most useful. They form the basis of other people's marriages.

LADY WINDERMERE'S FAN

Faithfulness is to the emotional life what consistency is to the life of the intellect – simply a confession of failure.

THE PICTURE OF DORIAN GRAY

. . . Living at the mercy of a woman who has neither mercy nor pity in her, a woman whom it is an infamy to meet, a degradation to know, a vile woman, a woman who comes between husband and wife!

LADY WINDERMERE'S FAN

My dear Count, for romantic young people like he is, the world always looks best at a distance.

VERA, OR THE NIHILISTS

Men marry because they are tired; women because they are curious. Both are disappointed.

A Woman of No Importance

My wife was very plain, never had my ruffs properly starched, and knew nothing of cookery.

The Canterville Ghost

You want a new excitement, Prince. Let me see – you have been married twice already; suppose you try falling in love for once.

Vera, or The Nihilists

When a woman marries again it is because she detested her first husband. When a man marries again, it is because he adored his first wife. Women try their luck; men risk theirs.

The Picture of Dorian Gray

He's entrammelled by this woman – fascinated by her – dominated by her. If a woman wants to hold a man, she has merely to appeal to what is worst in him.

Lady Windermere's Fan

Ah, nowadays people marry as often as they can, don't they? It is most fashionable.

An Ideal Husband

You talk as if you had a heart. Women like you have no hearts. Heart is not in you. You are bought and sold.

Lady Windermere's Fan

You seem to forget that I am married, and the one charm of marriage is that it makes a life of deception absolutely necessary for both parties.

The Picture of Dorian Gray

I know it is the general lot of women,
Each miserably mated to some man
Wrecks her own life upon his selfishness:
That it is general makes it not less bitter.
I think I never heard a woman laugh,
Laugh for pure merriment, except one woman,
That was at night time, in the public streets.
Poor soul, she walked with painted lips, and wore
The mask of pleasure: I would not laugh like her;
No, death were better.

THE DUCHESS OF PADUA

All men are married women's property. That is the only true definition of what married women's property really is.

A WOMAN OF NO IMPORTANCE

The annoying thing is that the wretches can be perfectly happy without us. That is why I think it is every woman's duty never to leave them alone for a single moment, except during this short breathing space after dinner; without which, I believe, we poor women would be absolutely worn to shadows.

A WOMAN OF NO IMPORTANCE

But we are positively getting elbowed into the corner. Our husbands would really forget our existence if we didn't nag at them from time to time, just to remind them that we have a perfect legal right to do so.

LADY WINDERMERE'S FAN

Egad! I might be married to her; she treats me with such demmed indifference.

LADY WINDERMERE'S FAN

The Ideal Husband? There couldn't be such a thing. The institution is wrong.

A WOMAN OF NO IMPORTANCE

Lord Caversham: What I say is that marriage is a matter for common sense.

Lord Goring: But women who have common sense are so curiously plain, father, aren't they? Of course I only speak from hearsay.

Lord Caversham: No woman, plain or pretty, has any common sense at all, sir. Common sense is the privilege of our sex.

AN IDEAL HUSBAND

There is always something ridiculous about the emotions of people whom one has ceased to love.

THE PICTURE OF DORIAN GRAY

The bond of all companionship, whether in marriage or in friendship, is conversation.

DE PROFUNDIS

More marriages are ruined nowadays by the common sense of the husband than by anything else.

A Woman of No Importance

Good heavens! How marriage ruins a man! It's as demoralising as cigarettes, and far more expensive.

Lady Windermere's Fan

Nothing ages a woman so rapidly as having married the general rule.

An Ideal Husband

You don't seem to realise, that in married life three is company and two is none.

The Importance of Being Earnest

To speak frankly, I am not in favour of long engagements. They give people the opportunity of finding out each other's characters before marriage, which I think is never advisable.

The Importance of Being Earnest

In married life affection comes when people thoroughly dislike each other.

An Ideal Husband

London is full of women who trust their husbands. One can always recognise them. They look so thoroughly unhappy.

Lady Windermere's Fan

Lord Caversham: If she did accept you she would be the prettiest fool in England.

Lord Goring: That is just what I should like to marry. A thoroughly sensible wife would reduce me to a condition of absolute idiocy in less than six months.

An Ideal Husband

Ah, all that I have noticed is that they are horribly tedious when they are good husbands, and abominably conceited when they are not.

A Woman of No Importance

Miss Prism: No married man is ever attractive except to his wife.

Chasuble: And often, I've been told, not even to her.

The Importance of Being Earnest

So much marriage is certainly not becoming. Twenty years of romance make a woman look like a ruin; but twenty years of marriage make her something like a public building.

A Woman of No Importance

Lord Illingworth: The Book of Life begins with a man and a woman in a garden.

Mrs. Allonby: It ends with Revelations.

A Woman of No Importance

Her sense of humour keeps her from the tragedy of a *grande passion*, and, as there is neither romance nor humility in her love, she makes an excellent wife.

The American Invasion

On the whole, the great success of marriage in the States is due, partly to the fact that no American man is ever idle, and partly to the fact that no American wife is considered responsible for the quality of her husband's dinners.

The American Man

He was eccentric, I admit. But only in later years. And that was the result of the Indian climate, and marriage, and indigestion, and other things of that kind.

The Importance of Being Earnest

My husband is a sort of promissory note; I'm tired of meeting him.

A Woman of No Importance

The real draw-back to marriage is that it makes one unselfish. And unselfish people are colourless. They lack individuality.

The Picture of Dorian Gray

From childhood, the husband has been brought up on the most elaborate fetch-and-carry system, and his reverence for the sex has a touch of compulsory chivalry about it, while the wife exercises an absolute despotism, based upon female assertion, and tempered by womanly charm.

THE AMERICAN MAN

To love oneself is the beginning of a lifelong romance.

AN IDEAL HUSBAND

It's perfectly scandalous the amount of bachelors who are going about society. There should be a law passed to compel them all to marry within twelve months.

A WOMAN OF NO IMPORTANCE

It is the growth of the moral sense of women that makes marriage such a hopeless, one-sided institution.

AN IDEAL HUSBAND

An engagement should come on a young girl as a surprise, pleasant or unpleasant, as the case may be.

THE IMPORTANCE OF BEING EARNEST

Those who are faithful know only the trivial side of love; it is the faithless who know love's tragedies.

THE PICTURE OF DORIAN GRAY

In America, the horrors of domesticity are almost entirely unknown. There are no scenes over the soup, no quarrels over the entrées, and as, by a clause inserted in every marriage settlement, the husband solemnly binds himself to use studs and not buttons for his shirts, one of the chief sources of disagreement in ordinary middle-class life is absolutely removed.

THE AMERICAN MAN

The proper basis for marriage is a mutual misunderstanding.

LORD ARTHUR SAVILE'S CRIME

A man can be happy with any woman as long as he does not love her.

THE PICTURE OF DORIAN GRAY

What a silly thing love is! It is not half as useful as logic, for it does not prove anything and it is always telling one things that are not going to happen, and making one believe things that are not true.

THE NIGHTINGALE AND THE ROSE

I have often observed that in married households the champagne is rarely of a first-rate brand.

THE IMPORTANCE OF BEING EARNEST

Loveless marriages are horrible. But there is one thing worse than an absolutely loveless marriage. A marriage in which there is love, but on one side only; faith, but on one side only; devotion, but on one side only and in which of the two hearts one is sure to be broken.

AN IDEAL HUSBAND

It's a curious thing. . . about the game of marriage – a game, by the way, that is going out of fashion – the wives hold all the honours, and invariably lose the odd trick.

LADY WINDERMERE'S FAN

It's most dangerous nowadays for a husband to pay any attention to his wife in public. It always makes people think that he beats her when they're alone.

LADY WINDERMERE'S FAN

One should always be in love. This is the reason one should never marry.

A WOMAN OF NO IMPORTANCE

By persistently remaining single a man converts himself into a permanent public temptation.

The Importance of Being Earnest

The happiness of a married man . . . depends on the people he has not married.

A Woman of No Importance

The Ideal Man should talk to us as if we were goddesses, and treat us as if we were children. He should refuse all our serious requests, and gratify every one of our whims. He should encourage us to have caprices, and forbid us to have missions. He should always say much more than he means, and always mean much more than he says.

A Woman of No Importance

I have always been of the opinion that a man who desires to get married should know either everything or nothing.

The Importance of Being Earnest

Civilised Society

Oh, I love London Society! I think it has immensely improved. It is entirely composed now of beautiful idiots and brilliant lunatics. Just what Society should be.

AN IDEAL HUSBAND

To get into the best society, nowadays, one has either to feed people, amuse people, or shock people – that is all!

A WOMAN OF NO IMPORTANCE

And now you must run away, for I am dining with some very dull people, who won't talk scandal, and I know that if I don't get my sleep now I shall never be able to keep awake during dinner.

LORD ARTHUR SAVILE'S CRIME

Society, civilised society at least, is never very ready to believe anything to the detriment of those who are both rich and fascinating. It feels instinctively that manners are of more importance than morals, and, in its opinion, the highest respectability is of much less value than the possession of a good chef.

THE PICTURE OF DORIAN GRAY

The fact is that our Society is terribly over-populated. Really, some one should arrange a proper scheme of assisted emigration. It would do a great deal of good.

An Ideal Husband

Yes, the public is wonderfully tolerant. It forgives everything except genius.

The Critic as Artist

Oh! talk to every woman as if you loved her, and to every man as if he bored you, and at the end of your first season, you will have the reputation of possessing the most perfect social tact.

A Woman of No Importance

Oh, your English society seems to me shallow, selfish, foolish. It has blinded its eyes, and stopped its ears. It lies like a leper in purple. It sits like a dead thing smeared with gold. It is all wrong, all wrong.

A Woman of No Importance

Charming ball it has been! Quite reminds me of old days. And I see that there are just as many fools in society as there used to be. So pleased to find that nothing has altered!

Lady Windermere's Fan

I always like the last person who is introduced to me; but, as a rule, as soon as I know people I get tired of them.

Lord Arthur Savile's Crime

We live in an age when unnecessary things are our only necessities.

The Picture of Dorian Gray

Never speak disrespectfully of Society, Algernon. Only people who can't get into it do that.

The Importance of Being Earnest

Lady Caroline: In my young days, Miss Worsley, one never met any one in society who worked for their living. It was not considered the thing.

Hester: In America those are the people we respect most.

Lady Caroline: I have no doubt of it.

A Woman of No Importance

Arguments are extremely vulgar, for everybody in good society holds exactly the same opinions.

The Remarkable Rocket

It is my last reception, and one wants something that will encourage conversation, particularly at the end of the season when everyone has practically said whatever they had to say, which, in most cases, was probably not much.

The Importance of Being Earnest

Society often forgives the criminal; it never forgives the dreamer.

The Critic as Artist

Can't make out how you stand London Society. The thing has gone to the dogs, a lot of damned nobodies talking about nothing.

An Ideal Husband

People nowadays are so absolutely superficial that they don't understand the philosophy of the superficial.

A Woman of No Importance

What is interesting about people in good Society is the mask that each one of them wears, not the reality that lies behind the mask.

The Decay of Lying

The public has always, and in every age, been badly brought up.

THE SOUL OF MAN UNDER SOCIALISM

Oh, I should fancy Mrs. Cheveley is one of those very modern women of our time who find a new scandal as becoming as a new bonnet, and air them both in the Park every afternoon at five-thirty.

AN IDEAL HUSBAND

Nothing is so dangerous as being too modern. One is apt to grow old-fashioned quite suddenly.

AN IDEAL HUSBAND

If it were not for the running-ground at Eton, the towing-path at Oxford, the Thames swimming baths, and the yearly circuses, humanity would forget the plastic perfection of its own form, and degenerate into a race of short-sighted professors, and spectacled *precieuses!*

LONDON MODELS

We live in the age of the over-worked, and under-educated; the age in which people are so industrious that they become absolutely stupid.

THE CRITIC AS ARTIST

A man who can dominate a London dinner-table can dominate the world. The future belongs to the dandy. It is the exquisites who are going to rule.

A Woman of No Importance

Oh! I don't care about the London season! It is too matrimonial. People are either hunting for husbands, or hiding from them.

An Ideal Husband

Lord Goring: Too much experience is a dangerous thing. Pray have a cigarette. Half the pretty women in London smoke cigarettes. Personally I prefer the other half.

Mrs. Cheveley: Thanks. I never smoke. My dressmaker wouldn't like it, and a woman's first duty is to her dressmaker, isn't it? What the second duty is, no one has as yet discovered.

An Ideal Husband

The security of Society lies in custom and unconscious instinct, and the basis of the stability of Society, as a healthy organism, is the complete absence of any intelligence amongst its members.

The Critic as Artist

Hester: I dislike London dinner-parties.

Mrs. Allonby: I adore them. The clever people never listen, and the stupid people never talk.

A Woman of No Importance

One is sure to be disappointed if one tries to get romance out of modern life.

Vera, or The Nihilists

It is absurd to divide people into good or bad. People are either charming or tedious.

Lady Windermere's Fan

One has never heard his name before in the whole course of one's life, which speaks volumes for a man, nowadays.

A Woman of No Importance

In literature mere egotism is delightful . . . Even in actual life egotism is not without its attractions. When people talk to us about others they are usually dull. When they talk to us about themselves they are nearly always interesting, and if one could shut them up, when they become wearisome, as easily as one can shut up a book of which one has grown wearied, they would be perfect absolutely.

The Critic as Artist

There is only one thing in the world worse than being talked about, and that is not being talked about.

The Picture of Dorian Gray

There is no reason why a man should show his life to the world. The world does not understand things.

De Profundis

It is perfectly monstrous the way people go about nowadays, saying things against one behind one's back that are absolutely true.

THE PICTURE OF DORIAN GRAY

Society takes upon itself the right to inflict appalling punishments on the individual, but it also has the supreme vice of shallowness, and fails to realise what it has done.

DE PROFUNDIS

Whenever people agree with me, I always feel I must be wrong.

LADY WINDERMERE'S FAN

I love scandals about other people, but scandals about myself don't interest me. They have not got the charm of novelty.

THE PICTURE OF DORIAN GRAY

If you pretend to be good, the world takes you very seriously. If you pretend to be bad, it doesn't. Such is the astounding stupidity of optimism.

LADY WINDERMERE'S FAN

The more one analyses people, the more all reasons for analysis disappear.

THE DECAY OF LYING

If there was less sympathy in the world there would be less trouble in the world.

DE PROFUNDIS

Most people are other people. Their thoughts are someone else's opinions, their life a mimicry, their passions a quotation.

DE PROFUNDIS

There is the same world for all of us, and good and evil, sin and innocence, go through it hand in hand.

LADY WINDERMERE'S FAN

Good people exasperate one's reason, bad people stir one's imagination.

DEFENCE OF DORIAN GRAY

All charming people, I fancy, are spoiled. It is the secret of their attraction.

THE PORTRAIT OF MR. W.H.

They drove me out to see the great prisons afterwards! Poor odd types of humanity in hideous striped dresses making bricks in the sun, and all mean-looking, which consoled me, for I should hate to see a criminal with a noble face.

LETTER TO HELENA SICKERT

The artist is always the munificent patron of the public. I am very fond of the public, and, personally, I always patronise the public very much.

INTERVIEW FOR *The Sketch*

I have always had grave suspicions that the basis of all literary cliques is a morbid love of meat teas. That makes them sadly uncivilised.

INTERVIEW FOR *The Sketch*

Exercise! The only possible form of exercise is to talk, not walk.

INTERVIEW FOR *The Sketch*

An Eloquent Fool

Learned conversation is either the affectation of the ignorant or the profession of the mentally unemployed.

THE CRITIC AS ARTIST

I am sick to death of cleverness. Everybody is clever nowadays. You can't go anywhere without meeting clever people. The thing has become an absolute public nuisance.

THE IMPORTANCE OF BEING EARNEST

We live in an age that reads too much to be wise, and that thinks too much to be beautiful.

THE PICTURE OF DORIAN GRAY

As a rule, I think they are quite impossible. Geniuses talk so much, don't they? Such a bad habit! And they are always thinking about themselves, when I want them to be thinking about me.

AN IDEAL HUSBAND

All thought is immoral. Its very essence is destruction. If you think of anything, you kill it. Nothing survives being thought of.

A WOMAN OF NO IMPORTANCE

The only people a painter should know... are people who are an artistic pleasure to look at and an intellectual repose to talk to.

THE MODEL MILLIONAIRE

It is only the intellectually lost who ever argue.

THE PICTURE OF DORIAN GRAY

And, as for what is called improving conversation, that is merely the foolish method by which the still more foolish philanthropist feebly tries to disarm the just rancour of the criminal classes.

THE CRITIC AS ARTIST

I do not approve of anything that tampers with natural ignorance. Ignorance is like a delicate exotic fruit; touch it and the bloom is gone.

THE IMPORTANCE OF BEING EARNEST

The only way to atone for being occasionally a little over-dressed is by being always absolutely over-educated.

PHRASES AND PHILOSOPHIES FOR THE USE OF THE YOUNG

There is no sin except stupidity.

THE CRITIC AS ARTIST

In examinations the foolish ask questions that the wise cannot answer.

PHRASES AND PHILOSOPHIES FOR THE USE OF THE YOUNG

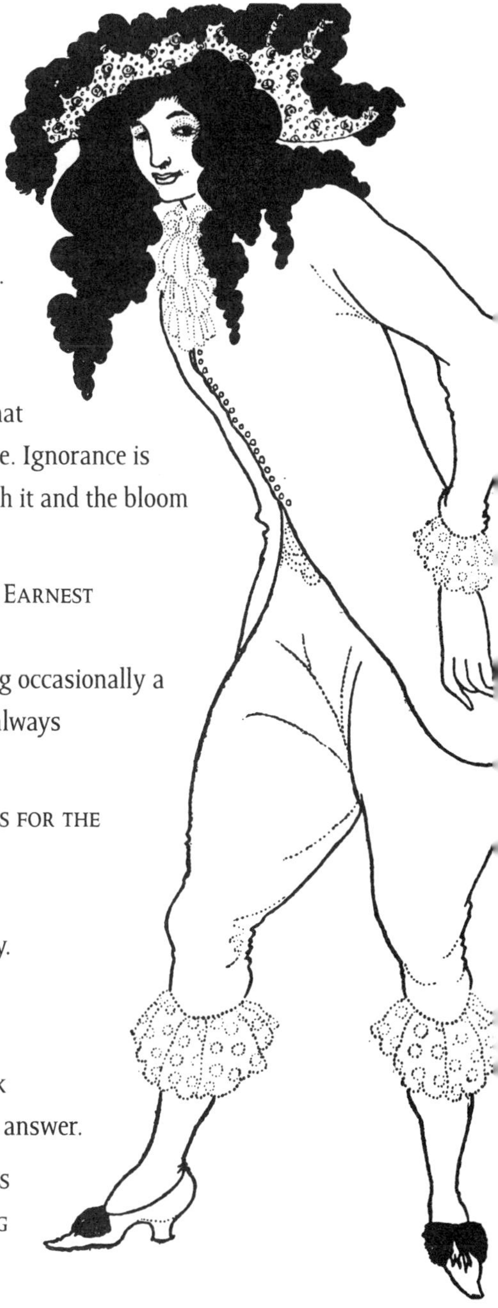

But oh! My dear Ernest, to sit next to a man who has spent his whole life in trying to educate others! What a dreadful experience that is!

The Critic as Artist

The English mind is always in a rage. The intellect of the race is wasted in the sordid and stupid quarrels of second-rate politicians or third-rate theologians.

The Critic as Artist

It is always an advantage not to have received a sound commercial education, and what I learned in the playing fields at Eton has been quite as useful to me as anything I was taught at Cambridge.

The Portrait of Mr. W.H.

Thinking is the most unhealthy thing in the world, and people die of it just as they die of any other disease. Fortunately, in England at any rate, thought is not catching.

The Decay of Lying

However, I think anything is better than high intellectual pressure. That is the most unbecoming thing there is. It makes the noses of the young girls so particularly large.

An Ideal Husband

Education is an admirable thing, but it is well to remember from time to time that nothing worth knowing can be taught.

THE CRITIC AS ARTIST

I am afraid that we are beginning to be over-educated; at least everybody who is incapable of learning has taken to teaching – that is really what our enthusiasm for education has come to.

THE DECAY OF LYING

But beauty, real beauty, ends where an intellectual expression begins.

AN IDEAL HUSBAND

I like looking at geniuses, and listening to beautiful people!

AN IDEAL HUSBAND

I am but too conscious of the fact that we are born in an age when only the dull are treated seriously, and I live in terror of not being understood.

THE CRITIC AS ARTIST

I like hearing myself talk. It is one of my greatest pleasures. I often have long conversations all by myself, and I am so clever that sometimes I don't understand a single word of what I am saying.

THE REMARKABLE ROCKET

The noblest character in the book is Lord Aubrey. As he is not a genius, he naturally behaves admirably on every occasion.

ON OUIDA'S NEW NOVEL [*Guilderoy*]

I am thoroughly sick of pearls. They make one look so plain, so good and so intellectual.

An Ideal Husband

I would not have about me shallow fools,
Who with mean scruples weigh the gold of life,
And faltering, paltering, end by failure.

The Duchess of Padua

Dullness is always an irresistible temptation for brilliancy, and stupidity is the permanent Bestia Trionfans that calls wisdom from its cave.

The Critic as Artist

But even men of the noblest possible moral character are extremely susceptible to the influence of the physical charms of others. Modern, no less than Ancient History, supplies us with many most painful examples of what I refer to. If it were not so, indeed, History would be quite unreadable.

The Importance of Being Earnest

People say that the schoolmaster is abroad. I wish to goodness he were.

The Critic as Artist

Bored by the tedious and improving conversation of those who have neither the wit to exaggerate nor the genius to romance...

The Decay of Lying

The whole theory of modern education is radically unsound. Fortunately in England, at any rate, education produces no effect whatsoever. If it did, it would prove a serious danger to the upper classes, and probably lead to acts of violence in Grosvenor Square.

THE IMPORTANCE OF BEING EARNEST

I am afraid that you have been listening to the conversation of someone older than yourself. That is always a dangerous thing to do, and if you allow it to degenerate into a habit, you will find it absolutely fatal to any intellectual development.

THE CRITIC AS ARTIST

Really, this horrid House of Commons quite ruins our husbands for us. I think the Lower House by far the greatest blow to a happy married life that there has been since that terrible thing called the Higher Education of Women was invented.

AN IDEAL HUSBAND

We all take such pains to over-educate ourselves. In the wild struggle for existence, we want to have something that endures, and so fill our minds with rubbish and facts, in the silly hope of keeping our place.

THE PICTURE OF DORIAN GRAY

I can stand brute force, but brute reason is quite unbearable. There is something unfair about its use. It is hitting below the intellect.

THE PICTURE OF DORIAN GRAY

The intellect is not a serious thing, and never has been. It is an instrument on which one plays, that is all. The only serious form of intellect I know is the British intellect. And on the British intellect the illiterates play the drum.

A WOMAN OF NO IMPORTANCE

Colonel: Can she read and write?

Peter: Ay, that she can, sir.

Colonel: Then she is a dangerous woman. No peasant should be allowed to do anything of the kind.

VERA, OR THE NIHILISTS

Ah! that quite does for me. I haven't a word to say... Too much care was taken with our education, I am afraid. To have been well brought up is a great drawback nowadays. It shuts one out from so much.

A Woman of No Importance

Lying for the sake of the improvement of the young, which is the basis of home education, still lingers amongst us.

The Decay of Lying

We teach people how to remember, we never teach them how to grow.

The Critic as Artist

Just as the philanthropist is the nuisance of the ethical sphere, so the nuisance of the intellectual sphere is the man who is so occupied in trying to educate others, that he has never had any time to educate himself.

The Critic as Artist

Intellect is in itself a mode of exaggeration, and destroys the harmony of any face.

The Picture of Dorian Gray

I adore simple pleasures. They are the last refuge of the complex.

A Woman of No Importance

The world has been made by fools that wise men should live in it!

A Woman of No Importance

Examinations are of no value whatsoever. If a man is a gentleman, he knows quite enough, and if he is not a gentleman, whatever he knows is bad for him.

A Woman of No Importance

Remember that the fool in the eyes of the gods and the fool in the eyes of man are very different.

De Profundis

But then no artist expects grace from the vulgar mind, or style from the suburban intellect.

The Soul of Man under Socialism

Women have become so highly educated . . . that nothing should surprise us nowadays, except happy marriages.

A Woman of No Importance

The man is but a very honest knave
Full of fine phrases for life's merchandise,
Selling most dear what he holds most cheap,
A windy brawler in a world of words.
I never met so eloquent a fool.

A Florentine Tragedy

The Grand Tour

The youth of America is their oldest tradition. It has been going on now for three hundred years. To hear them talk one would imagine they were in their first childhood. As far as civilisation goes they are in their second.

A WOMAN OF NO IMPORTANCE

American girls are as clever at concealing their parents as English women are at concealing their past.

THE PICTURE OF DORIAN GRAY

Lady Caroline: There are a great many things you haven't got in America, I am told, Miss Worsley. They say you have no ruins, and no curiosities.

Mrs Allonby: What nonsense! They have their mothers and their manners.

A WOMAN OF NO IMPORTANCE

We have really everything in common with America nowadays, except, of course, language.

THE CANTERVILLE GHOST

I am told that pork-packing is the most lucrative profession in America, after politics.

THE PICTURE OF DORIAN GRAY

The Rhine is of course tedious, the vineyards are formal and dull, and as far as I can judge, the inhabitants of Germany are American.

LETTER TO ROBERT ROSS

The English have a miraculous power to change wine into water.

[O.W. IN PARIS]

A typical Englishman, always dull and usually violent.

AN IDEAL HUSBAND

The British public are really not equal to the mental strain of having more than one topic every three months.

THE PICTURE OF DORIAN GRAY

If one could only teach the English how to talk, and the Irish how to listen, society here would be quite civilised.

AN IDEAL HUSBAND

The English country gentleman galloping after a fox – the unspeakable in full pursuit of the uneatable.

A Woman of No Importance

Do you know, Mr. Hopper, dear Agatha and I are so much interested in Australia. It must be so pretty with all the dear little kangaroos flying about. Agatha has found it on the map. What a curious shape it is! Just like a packing case.

Lady Windermere's Fan

To Australia? Oh, don't mention that dreadful vulgar place.

Lady Windermere's Fan

I trust you will return from Australia in a position of affluence. I believe there is no society of any kind in the Colonies, nothing that I would call society.

The Picture of Dorian Gray

One is impressed in America, but not favourably impressed, by the inordinate size of everything. The country seems to try to bully one into a belief in its power by its impressive bigness.

Impressions of America

American youths are pale and precocious, or sallow and supercilious, but American girls are pretty and charming – little oases of pretty unreasonableness in a vast desert of practical common-sense.

Impressions of America

The actual people who live
in Japan are not unlike
the general run of
English people; that is
to say, they are
extremely
commonplace, and have
nothing curious or
extraordinary about them.

THE DECAY OF LYING

Beer, the Bible, and the seven deadly virtues have made our England what she is.

THE PICTURE OF DORIAN GRAY

There are twenty ways of cooking a potato, and three hundred and sixty-four ways of cooking an egg, yet the British cook up to the present moment knows only three methods of sending up either one or the other.

DINNERS AND DISHES

I am not sure . . . that foreigners . . . should cultivate likes or dislikes about the people they are invited to meet.

A WOMAN OF NO IMPORTANCE

My dear General, your nephew must be a perfect Turk. He seems to get married three times a week regularly.

VERA, OR THE NIHILISTS

He talks of Europe as being old; but it is he himself who has never been young.

The American Man

On the whole, American girls have a wonderful charm, and, perhaps, the chief secret of their charm is that they never talk seriously, except to their dressmaker, and never think seriously, except about amusements.
They have, however, one grave fault – their mothers.

The American Invasion

America has never quite forgiven Europe for having been discovered somewhat earlier in history than itself.

THE AMERICAN MAN

La belle France is entirely ruined, Prince, through bad morals and worse cookery.

VERA, OR THE NIHILISTS

What a monstrous climate! . . . I guess the old country is so overpopulated that they have not enough decent weather for everybody. I have always been of opinion that emigration is the only thing for England.

THE CANTERVILLE GHOST

'I don't think I like American inventions, Arthur. I am quite sure I don't. I read some American novels lately, and they were quite nonsensical.

LORD ARTHUR SAVILE'S CRIME

Many American ladies on leaving their native land adopt an appearance of chronic ill-health, under the impression that it is a form of European refinement.

THE CANTERVILLE GHOST

The English people give intensely ugly names to places. One place had such an ugly name that I refused to lecture there. It was called Grigsville.

IMPRESSIONS OF AMERICA

It is true that when we meet him in Europe his conversation keeps us in fits of laughter; but this is merely because his ideas are so absolutely incongruous with European surroundings. Place him in his own environment... and the very same observations will fail to excite a smile. They have sunk to the level of the commonplace truism, or the sensible remark; and what seemed a paradox when we listened to it in London, becomes a platitude when we hear it in Milwaukee.

THE AMERICAN MAN

Freckles run in Scotch families just as gout does in English families.

THE PORTRAIT OF MR. W.H.

There are some who will welcome with delight the idea of solving the Irish problem by doing away with the Irish people.

ON *Mr. Froude's Blue Book* [ON IRELAND]

Once in New York, you are sure to be a great success. I know lots of people there who would give a hundred thousand dollars to have a grandfather, and much more than that to have a family ghost.

THE CANTERVILLE GHOST

The cities of America are inexpressibly tedious. The Bostonians take their learning too sadly; culture with them is an accomplishment rather than an atmosphere, their 'Hub', as they call it, is the paradise of prigs. Chicago is a sort of monster-shop, full of bustle and bores. Political life at Washington is like political life in a suburban vestry.

THE AMERICAN INVASION

Mrs. Allonby: They say, Lady Hunstanton, that when good Americans die they go to Paris.

Lady Hunstanton: Indeed? And when bad Americans die, where do they go to?

Lord Illingworth: Oh, they go to America.

A WOMAN OF NO IMPORTANCE

A nation arrayed in stove-pipe hats, and dress improvers, might have built the Pantechnicon, possibly, but the Parthenon, never.

THE RELATION OF DRESS TO ART

Salt Lake City contains only two buildings of note, the chief being the Tabernacle, which is the shape of a soup-kettle.

IMPRESSIONS OF AMERICA

If in the last century she [England] tried to govern Ireland with an insistence that was intensified by race-hatred and religious prejudice, she has sought to rule her in this century with a stupidity that is aggravated by good intentions.

ON *Mr. Froude's Blue Book* [ON IRELAND]

The English think that a cheque-book can solve every problem in life.

AN IDEAL HUSBAND

I can't stand your English house-parties. In England people actually try to be brilliant at breakfast. That is dreadful of them! Only dull people are brilliant at breakfast.

An Ideal Husband

Warned by the example of her mother that American women do not grow old gracefully, she tries not to grow old at all, and often succeeds.

The American Invasion

With the exception of the United States Minister, always a welcome personage wherever he goes, and an occasional lion from Boston or the Far West, no American man has any social existence in London.

THE AMERICAN INVASION

All Americans lecture, I believe. I suppose it is something in their climate.

A WOMAN OF NO IMPORTANCE

Dreary as were the old Pilgrim Fathers, who left our shores more than two centuries ago to found a New England beyond seas, the Pilgrim Mothers, who have returned to us in the nineteenth century, are drearier still. Here and there, of course, there are exceptions, but as a class they are either dull, dowdy, or dyspeptic.

THE AMERICAN INVASION

Hester (smiling) : We have the largest country in the world, Lady Caroline. They used to tell us at school that some of our states are as big as France and England put together.

Lady Caroline: Ah! you must find it very draughty, I should fancy.

A WOMAN OF NO IMPORTANCE

He had that curious love of green, which in individuals is always the sign of a subtle artistic temperament, and in nations is said to denote a laxity, if not a decadence of morals.

THE ARTIST AS CRITIC

I was disappointed with Niagara – most people must be disappointed with Niagara. Every American bride is taken there, and the sight of the stupendous waterfall must be one of the earliest, if not the keenest, disappointments in American married life.

IMPRESSIONS OF AMERICA

His one desire is to get the whole of Europe into thorough repair.

THE AMERICAN MAN

He is M. Renan's *l'homme sensuel moyen*, Mr. Arnold's middle-class Philistine. The telephone is his test of civilisation, and his wildest dreams of Utopia do not rise beyond elevated railways and electric bells.

THE AMERICAN MAN

UNADULTERATED COUNTRY LIFE

Anybody can be good in the country. There are no temptations there. That is the reason why people who live out of town are so absolutely uncivilised.

THE PICTURE OF DORIAN GRAY

Gwendolen: I had no idea there were any flowers in the country.

Cecily: Oh, flowers are as common here, Miss Fairfax, as people are in London.

THE IMPORTANCE OF BEING EARNEST

It is pure unadulterated country life. They get up early, because they have so much to do, and go to bed early because they have so little to think about.

THE PICTURE OF DORIAN GRAY

But somehow, I feel sure that if I lived in the country for six months, I should become so unsophisticated that no one would take the slightest notice of me.

A WOMAN OF NO IMPORTANCE

Nature has good intentions, of course, but, as Aristotle once said, she cannot carry them out.

THE DECAY OF LYING

Most women in London, nowadays, seem to furnish their rooms with nothing but orchids, foreigners, and French novels.

A WOMAN OF NO IMPORTANCE

Grass is hard and lumpy and damp, and full of dreadful black insects. Why, even Morris' poorest workman could make you a more comfortable seat than the whole of Nature can.

THE DECAY OF LYING

One of those utterly tedious amusements one only finds at an English country house on an English country Sunday.

The Picture of Dorian Gray

When one is in town one amuses oneself. When one is in the country one amuses other people.

The Importance of Being Earnest

If Nature had been comfortable, mankind would never have invented architecture, and I prefer houses to the open air.

The Decay of Lying

What Art really reveals to us is Nature's lack of design, her curious crudities, her extraordinary monotony, her absolutely unfinished condition.

The Decay of Lying

Like most artificial people he had a love of nature.

Pen, Pencil and Poison

Egotism itself, which is so necessary to a proper sense of dignity, is entirely the result of indoor life. Out of doors one becomes abstract and impersonal.

The Decay of Lying

Land has ceased to be either a profit or a pleasure. It gives one position, and prevents one from keeping it up.

The Importance of Being Earnest

You have a town house, I hope? A girl with a simple, unspoiled nature, like Gwendolen, could hardly be expected to reside in the country.

THE IMPORTANCE OF BEING EARNEST

Gwendolen: Personally I cannot understand how anybody manages to exist in the country, if anybody who is anybody does. The country always bores me to death.

Cecily: Ah! This is what the newspapers call agricultural depression, is it not? I believe the aristocracy are suffering very much from it just at present.

THE IMPORTANCE OF BEING EARNEST

As for the infinite variety of Nature, that is a pure myth. It is not to be found in Nature herself. It resides in the imagination, or fancy, or cultivated blindness of the man who looks at her.

THE DECAY OF LYING

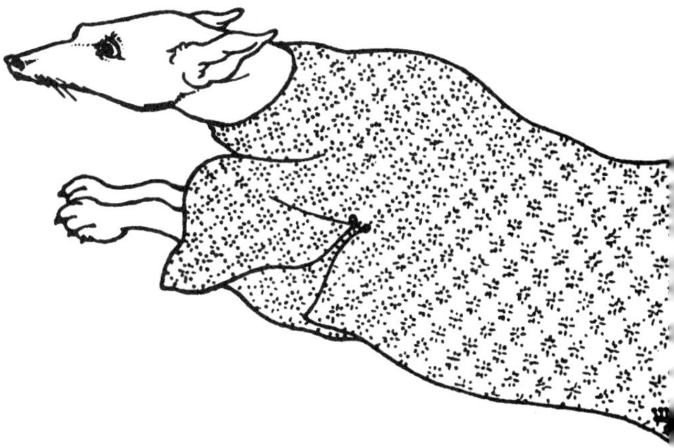

London is too full of fogs and . . . serious people . . . Whether the fogs produce the serious people or whether the serious people produce the fogs, I don't know . . .

LADY WINDERMERE'S FAN

You have nothing to look at but chimney-pot hats, men with sandwich boards, vermilion letterboxes, and do that at the risk of being run over by an emerald-green omnibus.

LECTURE TO ART STUDENTS

And then look at the depressing, monotonous appearance of any modern city, the sombre dress of men and women, the meaningless and barren architecture, the colourless and dreadful surroundings.

LECTURE TO ART STUDENTS

Art is very difficult in this unlovely town of ours, where, as you go to work in the mornings, or return from it at eventide, you have to pass through street after street of the most foolish and stupid architecture that the world has ever seen; architecture . . . reducing three-fourths of the London houses to being, merely, like square boxes of the vilest proportions, as gaunt as they are grimy, and as poor as they are pretentious.

LECTURE TO ART STUDENTS

A man who can dominate a London dinner-table can dominate the world.

A WOMAN OF NO IMPORTANCE

RELATIVE VALUES

Children begin by loving their parents. After a time they judge them. Rarely, if ever, do they forgive them.

A Woman of No Importance

Fathers should be neither seen nor heard. That is the only proper basis for family life.

An Ideal Husband

Oh, brothers! I don't care for brothers. My elder brother won't die, and my younger brothers seem never to do anything else.

The Picture of Dorian Gray

And now that I think of it I have never heard any man mention his brother. The subject seems distasteful to most men.

The Importance of Being Earnest

It is a ridiculous attachment . . . she has no money, and far too many relations.

The Happy Prince

No one cares about distant relatives nowadays. They went out of fashion years ago.

Lord Arthur Savile's Crime

A family is a terrible incumbrance, especially when one is not married.

Vera, or The Nihilists

After a good dinner one can forgive anybody, even one's relations.

A Woman of No Importance

As for domesticity, it ages one rapidly, and distracts one's mind from higher things.

The Remarkable Rocket

It is a very dangerous thing to know one's friends.

The Remarkable Rocket

What is the good of friendship if one cannot say exactly what one means? Anybody can say charming things and try to please and flatter, but a true friend always says unpleasant things, and does not mind giving pain.

The Devoted Friend

I seem to have heard that observation before, Ernest. It has all the vitality of error and all the tediousness of an old friend.

The Critic as Artist

I can't help detesting my relations. I suppose it comes from the fact that none of us can stand other people having the same faults as ourselves.

The Picture of Dorian Gray

I think that generosity is the essence of friendship.

The Devoted Friend

The American father is better, for he is never in London. He passes his life entirely in Wall Street, and communicates with his family once a month by means of a telegram in cipher. The mother, however, is always with us, and, lacking the quick imitative faculty of the younger generation, remains uninteresting and provincial to the last.

THE AMERICAN INVASION

Relations are simply a tedious pack of people, who haven't got the remotest knowledge of how to live, nor the smallest instinct about when to die.

THE IMPORTANCE OF BEING EARNEST

I was in hopes he would have married Lady Kelso. But I believe he said her family was too large. Or was it her feet? I forget which.

A WOMAN OF NO IMPORTANCE

The home seems to me to be the proper sphere for the man. And certainly once a man begins to neglect his domestic duties he becomes painfully effeminate, does he not? And I don't like that. It makes men so very attractive.

THE IMPORTANCE OF BEING EARNEST

Women should not be idle in their homes.
For idle fingers make a thoughtless heart.

A FLORENTINE TRAGEDY

Her mother is perfectly unbearable. Never met such a Gorgon . . .

THE IMPORTANCE OF BEING EARNEST

Lord Illingworth: People's mothers always bore me to death. All women become like their mothers. That is their tragedy.

Mrs. Allonby: No man does. That is his.

A WOMAN OF NO IMPORTANCE

To lose one parent, Mr. Worthing may be regarded as a misfortune; to lose both looks like carelessness.

THE IMPORTANCE OF BEING EARNEST

As long as a woman can look ten years younger than her daughter, she is perfectly satisfied.

THE PICTURE OF DORIAN GRAY

'But when I think that they may lose their only son, I certainly am very much affected.'
'You certainly are!' cried the Bengal Light. 'In fact, you are the most affected person I ever met.'

THE REMARKABLE ROCKET

I choose my friends for their good looks, my acquaintances for their good characters, and my enemies for their good intellects. A man cannot be too careful in the choice of his enemies.

THE PICTURE OF DORIAN GRAY

It is always painful to part from people whom one has known for a very brief space of time. The absence of old friends one can endure with equanimity. But even a momentary separation from anyone to whom one has just been introduced is almost unbearable.

THE IMPORTANCE OF BEING EARNEST

Good novelists are much rarer than good sons.

ON A NEW BOOK ON DICKENS

Now, Tuppy, you've lost your figure and you've lost your character. Don't lose your temper; you have only got one.

LADY WINDERMERE'S FAN

What on earth you are serious about I haven't got the remotest idea. About everything, I should fancy. You have such an absolutely trivial nature.

THE IMPORTANCE OF BEING EARNEST

Laughter is not at all a bad beginning for a friendship, and is far the best ending for one.

THE PICTURE OF DORIAN GRAY

I dare say that if I knew him I should not be his friend at all. It is a very dangerous thing to know one's friends.

THE REMARKABLE ROCKET

Anybody can sympathise with the sufferings of a friend, but it requires a very fine nature to sympathise with a friend's success.

THE SOUL OF MAN UNDER SOCIALISM

I always like to know everything about my new friends, and nothing about my old ones.

THE PICTURE OF DORIAN GRAY

I love hearing my relations abused. It is the only thing that makes me put up with them at all.

THE IMPORTANCE OF BEING EARNEST

The Prettiest Of Playthings

You were the prettiest of playthings, the most fascinating of small romances.

A Woman of No Importance

The only way a woman can ever reform a man is by boring him so completely that he loses all possible interest in life.

The Picture of Dorian Gray

A woman will flirt with anybody in the world as long as other people are looking on.

The Picture of Dorian Gray

She wore far too much rouge last night, and not quite enough clothes. That is always a sign of despair in a woman.

An Ideal Husband

She is a peacock in everything but beauty.

The Picture of Dorian Gray

Women represent the triumph of matter over mind – just as men represent the triumph of mind over morals.

A Woman of No Importance

Men who are dandies and women who are darlings rule the world.

THE MODEL MILLIONAIRE

Women, as some witty Frenchman once put it, inspire us with the desire to do masterpieces, and always prevent us from carrying them out.

THE PICTURE OF DORIAN GRAY

Women are meant to be loved, not to be understood.

THE SPHINX WITHOUT A SECRET

When a man does exactly what a woman expects him to do she doesn't think much of him. One should always do what a woman doesn't expect, just as one should say what she doesn't understand.

THE IMPORTANCE OF BEING EARNEST

The only way to behave to a woman is to make love to her, if she is pretty, and to someone else, if she is plain.

THE IMPORTANCE OF BEING EARNEST

Women have a wonderful instinct about things. They can discover everything except the obvious.

AN IDEAL HUSBAND

She was perfectly proportioned – a rare thing in an age when so many women are either over life-size or insignificant.

LORD ARTHUR SAVILE'S CRIME

Like all stout women, she looks the very picture of happiness.

An Ideal Husband

Many a woman has a past, but I am told that she has at least a dozen, and that they all fit.

Lady Windermere's Fan

My dear Margaret, what a handsome woman your husband has been dancing with! I should be quite jealous if I were you! Is she a great friend of yours?

Lady Windermere's Fan

You women live by your emotions and for them. You have no philosophy of life.

A Woman of No Importance

Lady Plymdale: Who is that well-dressed woman talking to Windermere?

Dumby: Haven't got the slightest idea! Looks like an *edition de luxe* of a wicked French novel, meant specially for the English market.

Lady Windermere's Fan

It takes a thoroughly good woman to do a thoroughly stupid thing.

Lady Windermere's Fan

I always liked your taste in wine and wives extremely.

Vera, or The Nihilists

The history of women is the history of the worst form of tyranny the world has ever known. The tyranny of the weak over the strong.

A Woman of No Importance

Jack: I'll bet you anything you like that half an hour after they have met, they will be calling each other sister.

Algernon: Women only do that when they have called each other a lot of other things first.

The Importance of Being Earnest

You should never try to understand them. Women are pictures. Men are problems. If you want to know what a woman really means – which, by the way, is always a dangerous thing to do – look at her, don't listen to her.

A Woman of No Importance

Ordinary women never appeal to one's imagination. They are limited to their century. No glamour ever transfigures them. One knows their minds as easily as one knows their bonnets.

The Picture of Dorian Gray

Women are a fascinatingly wilful sex. Every woman is a rebel, and usually in wild revolt against herself.

A Woman of No Importance

A man's life is of more value than a woman's. It has larger issues, wider scope, greater ambitions.

AN IDEAL HUSBAND

I am afraid that women appreciate cruelty, downright cruelty, more than anything else. They have wonderfully primitive instincts. We have emancipated them, but they remain slaves looking for their masters all the same. They love being dominated.

THE PICTURE OF DORIAN GRAY

These straw-coloured women have dreadful tempers.

LADY WINDERMERE'S FAN

The one charm of the past is that it is past. But women never know when the curtain has fallen. They always want a sixth act, and as soon as the interest in the play is entirely over they propose to continue it.

THE PICTURE OF DORIAN GRAY

Oh! Wicked women bother one. Good women bore one. That is the difference between them.

LADY WINDERMERE'S FAN

She certainly has a wonderful faculty of remembering people's names and forgetting their faces.

A Woman of No Importance

Women have no appreciation of good looks; at least, good women have not.

The Picture of Dorian Gray

We women adore failures. They lean on us.

A Woman of No Importance

Curious thing, plain women are always jealous of their husbands, beautiful women never are!

A Woman of No Importance

You flatter her.
She has her virtues as most women have,
But beauty is a gem she may not wear.

A Florentine Tragedy

But good women have such limited views of life, their horizon is so small, their interests so petty.

A Woman of No Importance

What a typical woman you are! You talk sentimentally and you are thoroughly selfish the whole time.

A Woman of No Importance

In the art of amusing men they are adepts, both by nature and education, and can actually tell a story without forgetting the point – an accomplishment that is extremely rare among the women of other countries.

THE AMERICAN INVASION

Women are never disarmed by compliments. Men always are. That is the difference between the two sexes.

AN IDEAL HUSBAND

Crying is the refuge of plain women, but the ruin of pretty ones.

LADY WINDERMERE'S FAN

If a woman really repents, she has to go to a bad dressmaker, otherwise no one believes in her.

LADY WINDERMERE'S FAN

In the case of very fascinating women, sex is a challenge, not a defence.

AN IDEAL HUSBAND

One should never give a woman anything she can't wear in the evening.

AN IDEAL HUSBAND

Young women of the present day seem to make it the sole object of their lives to be always playing with fire.

A WOMAN OF NO IMPORTANCE

She has not touched the tambour frame for nine or ten years. But she has many other amusements. She is very much interested in her own health.

A WOMAN OF NO IMPORTANCE

I don't think man has much capacity for development. He has got as far as he can, and that is not far, is it?

AN IDEAL HUSBAND

Men become old, but they never become good.

LADY WINDERMERE'S FAN

The world was made for men and not for women.

A WOMAN OF NO IMPORTANCE

If a woman wants to hold a man, she has merely to appeal to the worst in him.

Lady Windermere's Fan

Man, poor, awkward, reliable, necessary man belongs to a sex that has been rational for millions and millions of years. He can't help himself.

A Woman of No Importance

Young men want to be faithful, and are not; old men want to be faithless, and cannot.

The Picture of Dorian Gray

No man has real success in this world unless he has got a woman to back him, and women rule society.

A Woman of No Importance

The fact is that men should never try to dictate to women. They never know how to do it, and when they do it, they always say something particularly foolish.

The Importance of Being Earnest

I like men who have a future, and women who have a past.

The Picture of Dorian Gray

Some Useful Professions

There is something tragic about the enormous number of young men there are in England at the present moment who start life with perfect profiles, and end by adopting some useful profession.

PHRASES AND PHILOSOPHIES FOR THE USE OF THE YOUNG

I have no sympathy myself with industry of any kind, least of all with such industries as you seem to recommend. Indeed, I have always been of the opinion that hard work is simply the refuge of people who have nothing whatever to do.

THE REMARKABLE ROCKET

It is very vulgar to talk about one's business. Only people like stockbrokers do that, and then merely at dinner parties.

THE IMPORTANCE OF BEING EARNEST

He had gone on the Stock Exchange for six months; but what was a butterfly to do among bulls and bears?

THE MODEL MILLIONAIRE

If you have not got women on your side you are quite over. You might just as well be a barrister or a stockbroker, or a journalist at once.

A WOMAN OF NO IMPORTANCE

The fact is, that civilisation requires slaves. The Greeks were quite right there. Unless there are slaves to do the ugly, horrible, uninteresting work, culture and contemplation become almost impossible.

THE SOUL OF MAN UNDER SOCIALISM

In England a man who can't talk morality twice a week to a large, popular, immoral audience is quite over as a serious politician. There would be nothing left for him as a profession except Botany or the Church.

AN IDEAL HUSBAND

We in the House of Lords are never in touch with public opinion. That makes us a civilised body.

A WOMAN OF NO IMPORTANCE

My dear father, only people who look dull ever get into the House of Commons, and only people who are dull ever succeed there.

AN IDEAL HUSBAND

You forget we are diplomatists. Men of thought should have nothing to do with action. Reforms in Russia are very tragic, but they always end in a farce.

VERA, OR THE NIHILISTS

There is nothing necessarily dignified about manual labour at all, and most of it is absolutely degrading.

THE SOUL OF MAN UNDER SOCIALISM

Lady Basildon: I delight in talking politics. I talk them all day long. But I can't bear listening to them. I don't know how the unfortunate men in the House stand these long debates.

Lord Goring: By never listening.

AN IDEAL HUSBAND

There is hardly a single person in the House of Commons worth painting; though many of them would be better for a little white-washing.

THE PICTURE OF DORIAN GRAY

She ultimately was so broken-hearted that she went into a convent, or on to the operatic stage, I forget which. No; I think it was decorative art-needlework she took up. I know she had lost all sense of pleasure in life.

AN IDEAL HUSBAND

And when scientific men are no longer called upon to go down to a depressing East-end and distribute cocoa and worse blankets to starving people, they will have delightful leisure in which to devise wonderful and marvellous things for their own joy and the joy of everyone else.

THE SOUL OF MAN UNDER SOCIALISM

The English detectives are really our best friends, and I have always found that by relying on their stupidity, we can do exactly what we like.

LORD ARTHUR SAVILE'S CRIME

Jack: My dear Algy, you talk exactly as if you were a dentist. It is very vulgar to talk like a dentist when one isn't a dentist. It produces a false impression.

Algernon: Well, that is exactly what dentists always do.

THE IMPORTANCE OF BEING EARNEST

A publicist, nowadays, is a man who bores the community with the details of the illegalities of his private life.

THE CRITIC AS ARTIST

A publisher is simply a useful middle-man.

DEFENCE OF DORIAN GRAY

To give an accurate description of what has never occurred is not merely the proper occupation of the historian, but the inalienable privilege of any man of parts and culture.

THE CRITIC AS ARTIST

They say a good lawyer can break the law as often as he likes, and no one can say him nay.

VERA, OR THE NIHILISTS

Then there were some arrows, barbed and brilliant, shot off, with all the speed and splendour of fireworks, at the archaeologists, who spend their lives in verifying the birth-places of nobodies, and estimate the value of a work of art by its date or by its decay, at the art critics who always treat a picture as if it were a novel, and try and find out the plot . . .

MR. WHISTLER'S TEN O'CLOCK

A cook and a diplomatist! An excellent parallel. If I had a son who was a fool I'd make him one or the other.

VERA, OR THE NIHILISTS

For myself, the only immortality I desire is to invent a new sauce.

VERA, OR THE NIHILISTS

Industry is the root of all ugliness.

PHRASES AND PHILOSOPHIES FOR THE USE OF THE YOUNG

The real difficulty, however, that we all have to face in life, is not so much the science of cookery, as the stupidity of cooks.

DINNERS AND DISHES

For the British cook is a foolish woman, who should be turned, for her iniquities, into a pillar of that salt which she never knows how to use.

DINNERS AND DISHES

It is the Philistine who seeks to estimate a personality by the vulgar test of production.

PEN, PENCIL AND POISON

Let me say to you now that to do nothing at all is the most difficult thing in the world, the most difficult thing and the most intellectual.

THE CRITIC AS ARTIST

Lying for the sake of a monthly salary is of course well-known in Fleet Street, and the profession of a political leader-writer is not without its advantages. But it is said to be a somewhat dull occupation, and it certainly does not lead to much beyond a kind of ostentatious obscurity.

THE DECAY OF LYING

One must have some occupation nowadays. If I hadn't my debts I shouldn't have anything to think about.

A WOMAN OF NO IMPORTANCE

Let me assure you that if I had not always had an entrée to the very best society, and the very worst conspiracies, I could never have been Prime Minister in Russia.

VERA, OR THE NIHILISTS

Sir John's temper since he has taken seriously to politics has become quite unbearable. Really, now that the House of Commons is trying to become useful, it does a great deal of harm.

AN IDEAL HUSBAND

I assure you my life will be quite ruined unless they send John at once to the Upper House. He won't take any interest in politics then, will he? The House of Lords is so sensible. An assembly of gentlemen.

AN IDEAL HUSBAND

Ambition is the last refuge of the failure.

PHRASES AND PHILOSOPHIES FOR THE USE OF THE YOUNG

Besides the professional posers of the studio there are posers of the Row, the posers at afternoon teas, the posers in politics and the circus posers. All four classes are delightful, but only the last class is ever really decorative.

LONDON MODELS

The salesman . . . knows nothing of what he is selling save that he is charging too much for it.

HOUSE DECORATION

Unsound Art

They afterwards took me to a dancing saloon where I saw the only rational method of art criticism I have ever come across. Over the piano was printed a notice:–
'Please do not shoot the pianist. He is doing his best.'

IMPRESSIONS OF AMERICA

I like Wagner's music better than anybody's. It is so loud that one can talk the whole time without people hearing what one says.

THE PICTURE OF DORIAN GRAY

Lady Hunstanton: Music makes one feel so romantic – at least it always gets on one's nerves.
Mrs Allonby: It's the same thing, nowadays.

A WOMAN OF NO IMPORTANCE

It is only an auctioneer who should admire all schools of art.

TO READ, OR NOT TO READ

There is nothing of the specialist in Mr. Whistler. . . He has done etchings with the brilliancy of epigrams, and pastels with the charm of paradoxes, and many of his portraits are pure works of fiction.

THE BUTTERFLY BOSWELL

For an artist to marry his model is as fatal as for a gourmet to marry his cook, the one gets no sittings, and the other gets no dinners.

LONDON MODELS

The English models are a well-behaved and hard-working class, and if they are much more interested in artists than they are in art, a large section of the public is in the same condition, and most of our modern exhibitions seem to justify its choice.

London Models

One should either be a work of art, or wear a work of art.

Phrases and Philosophies for the Use of the Young

As a rule, people who act lead the most commonplace life.

The Picture of Dorian Gray

We are sorry too to find an English dramatic critic misquoting Shakespeare, as we had always been of the opinion that this was a privilege reserved specially for our English actors.

A Cheap Edition of a Great Man

It is a consolation to know, however, that such an artist as Madame Bernhardt has not only worn that yellow, ugly dress, but has been photographed in it.

IMPRESSIONS OF AMERICA

In a very ugly and sensible age, the arts borrow, not from life, but from each other.

THE DECAY OF LYING

Musical people are so absurdly unreasonable. They always want one to be perfectly dumb at the very moment when one is longing to be absolutely deaf.

AN IDEAL HUSBAND

No; I don't want music at present. It is far too indefinite. Besides, I took the Baroness Bernstein down to dinner last night, and, though absolutely charming in every other respect, she insisted on discussing music as if it were actually written in the German language.

THE CRITIC AS ARTIST

There are moments when Art almost attains to the dignity of manual labour.

THE MODEL MILLIONAIRE

People are so annoying. All my pianists look exactly like poets; and all my poets look exactly like pianists.

LORD ARTHUR SAVILE'S CRIME

For that he [Whistler] is indeed one of the very greatest masters of painting, is my opinion. And I may add that in this opinion Mr. Whistler himself entirely concurs.

Mr. Whistler's Ten O'Clock

An artist's heart is in his head.

The Model Millionaire

Most of our elderly English painters spend their wicked and wasted lives in poaching upon the domain of the poets, marring their motives by clumsy treatment, and striving to render, by visible form or colour, the marvel of what is invisible, the splendour of what is not seen.

The Critic as Artist

If one plays good music people don't listen, and if one plays bad music people don't talk.

The Importance of Being Earnest

After playing Chopin, I feel as if I had been weeping over sins that I had never committed, and mourning over tragedies that were not my own. Music always seems to produce that effect.

The Critic as Artist

Whatever music sounds like, I am glad to say that it does not sound in the smallest degree like German.

The Critic as Artist

I never talk during music, at least during good music. If one hears bad music, it is one's duty to drown it in conversation.

THE PICTURE OF DORIAN GRAY

Mediocrity weighing mediocrity in the balance, and incompetence applauding its brother – that is the spectacle which the artistic activity of England affords us from time to time.

THE CRITIC AS ARTIST

They have degraded the visible arts into the obvious arts, and the one thing not worth looking at is the obvious.

THE CRITIC AS ARTIST

Last night, at Prince's Hall, Mr. Whistler made his first public appearance as a lecturer on art, and spoke for more than an hour with really marvellous eloquence on the absolute uselessness of all lectures of the kind.

Mr. Whistler's Ten O'Clock

As long as a painter is a painter merely, he should not be allowed to talk of anything but mediums and megilp, and on those subjects should be compelled to hold his tongue.

Mr. Whistler's Ten O'Clock

The domestic virtues are not the true basis of art, though they may serve as an excellent advertisement for second-rate artists.

The Critic as Artist

Well, I found myself seated in a horrid little private box, with a vulgar drop-scene staring me in the face. I looked out from behind the curtain, and surveyed the house. It was a tawdry affair, all Cupids and cornucopias, like a third-rate wedding cake.

The Picture of Dorian Gray

As for Sir Frederick Leighton, he has rarely been seen to more advantage than in the specimen of his work that Mr. Furniss has so kindly provided for him. His 'Pygmalion and Galatea in the Lowther Arcadia' (No. 49) has all that wax-doll grace of treatment that is so characteristic of his best work, and is eminently suggestive of the President's earnest and continual struggles to discover the difference between chalk and colour.

THE ROUT OF THE R[OYAL] A[CADEMY]

Mr. Frith, who has done so much to elevate painting to the dignity of photography, sends a series of five pictures exemplifying that difference between Virtue and Vice which moralists have never been able to discover, but which is the real basis of the great Drury Lane school of melodrama . . . The whole series is like the very finest platitude from the pulpit, and shows clearly the true value of didactic art.

THE ROUT OF THE R[OYAL] A[CADEMY]

That an artist will find beauty in ugliness, *le beau dans l'horrible*, is now a commonplace of the schools, the argot of the atelier, but I strongly deny that charming people should be condemned to live with magenta ottomans and Albert blue curtains in their rooms in order that some painter may observe the side lights on the one and the values of the other.

MR. WHISTLER'S TEN O'CLOCK

She is like most artists; she is all style without any sincerity.

THE NIGHTINGALE AND THE ROSE

The moral life of man forms part of the subject-matter of the artist, but the morality of art consists in the perfect use of an imperfect medium.

THE PICTURE OF DORIAN GRAY

Bad artists always admire each other's work. They call it being large-minded and free from prejudice.

THE CRITIC AS ARTIST

In art good intentions are not the smallest value. All bad art is the result of good intentions.

DE PROFUNDIS

I don't play accurately – anyone can play accurately – but I play with wonderful expression. As far as the piano is concerned, sentiment is my forte. I keep science for Life.

THE IMPORTANCE OF BEING EARNEST

This unfortunate aphorism about Art holding the mirror up to Nature is deliberately said by Hamlet in order to convince the bystanders of his absolute insanity in all art-matters.

THE DECAY OF LYING

We can forgive a man for making a useful thing as long as he does not admire it. The only excuse for making a useless thing is that one admires it intensely. All art is quite useless.

THE PICTURE OF DORIAN GRAY

In fairness to the audience, however, I must say that they seemed extremely gratified at being rid of the dreadful responsibility of admiring anything, and nothing could have exceeded their enthusiasm when they were told by Mr. Whistler that no matter how vulgar their dresses were, or how hideous their surroundings at home, still it was possible that a great painter, if there was such a thing, could, by contemplating them in the twilight, and half-closing his eyes, see them under really picturesque conditions, and produce a picture which they were not to attempt to understand, much less to enjoy.

MR. WHISTLER'S TEN O'CLOCK

It is the spectator, and not life, that art really mirrors.

THE PICTURE OF DORIAN GRAY

Admirable as are Mr. Whistler's fire-works on canvas, his fire-works in prose are abrupt, violent and exaggerated.

THE NEW PRESIDENT [OF THE ROYAL SOCIETY OF BRITISH ARTISTS]

Art never expresses anything but itself.

THE DECAY OF LYING

The public clung with really pathetic tenacity to what I believe were the direct traditions of the Great Exhibition of international vulgarity, traditions that were so appalling that the houses in which people lived were only fit for blind people to live in.

THE SOUL OF MAN UNDER SOCIALISM

All bad art comes from returning to Life and Nature, and elevating them into ideals.

THE DECAY OF LYING

As a method Realism is a complete failure, and the two things that every artist should avoid are modernity of form and modernity of subject-matter.

THE DECAY OF LYING

The moment that an artist takes notice of what other people want, and tries to supply the demand, he ceases to be an artist, and becomes a dull or an amusing craftsman, an honest or dishonest tradesman.

THE SOUL OF MAN UNDER SOCIALISM

Trevor was a painter. Indeed, few people escape that nowadays.

THE MODEL MILLIONAIRE

Art is the most intense mode of individualism that the world has ever known.

The Soul of Man under Socialism

An artist, sir, has no ethical sympathies at all. Virtue and wickedness are to him simply what the colours in his palette are to the painter.

Defence of Dorian Gray

The English public, as a mass, takes no interest in a work of art until it is told that the work in question is immoral.

Defence of Dorian Gray

In New York, and even in Boston, a good model is so great a rarity that most of the artists are reduced to painting Niagara and millionaires.

London Models

Mr. Bought's 'Newest England, Tarred with an American Brush,' is, as the catalogue remarks, somewhat low in tone, though high in price.

The Rout of the R[oyal] A[cademy]

Elsewhere on the walls of this delightful exhibition we notice . . . the Leslies and the Marcus Stones have all that faint and fading prettiness that makes us long for the honest ugliness of naturalism; of the work of that poetic school of artists, who imagine that the true way of idealising a sitter is to paint the portrait of somebody else.

The Rout of the R[oyal] A[cademy]

On the whole, then, the Royal Academicians have never appeared under more favourable conditions than in this pleasant gallery. Mr. Furniss has shown that the one thing lacking in them is a sense of humour, and that, if they would not take themselves so seriously, they might produce work that would be a joy, and not a weariness, to the world. Whether or not they will profit by the lesson, it is difficult to say, for dullness has become the basis of respectability, and seriousness the only refuge of the shallow.

THE ROUT OF THE R[OYAL] A[CADEMY]

Mr. Whistler always spelt art, and we believe still spells it, with a capital 'I'. However, he was never dull. His brilliant wit, his caustic satire, and his amusing epigrams, or perhaps we should say epitaphs on his contemporaries made his views on art as delightful as they were misleading, and as fascinating as they were unsound.

THE NEW PRESIDENT [OF THE ROYAL SOCIETY OF BRITISH ARTISTS]

SECOND RATE SONNETS

Inferior poets are absolutely fascinating. The worse their rhymes are, the more picturesque they look. The mere fact of having published a book of second-rate sonnets makes a man quite irresistible. He lives the poetry that he cannot write.

THE PICTURE OF DORIAN GRAY

Lying and poetry are arts – arts, as Plato saw, not unconnected with each other – and they require the most careful study, the most disinterested devotion.

THE DECAY OF LYING

I hate vulgar realism in literature. The man who could call a spade a spade should be compelled to use one. It is the only thing he is fit for.

THE PICTURE OF DORIAN GRAY

Anybody can write a three-volumed novel. It merely requires a complete ignorance of both life and literature.

THE CRITIC AS ARTIST

On a lazy June evening no more delightful companion could be found than a poet who has the sweetest of voices and absolutely nothing to say.

POETRY AND PRISON

Books of poetry by young writers are usually promissory notes that are never met.

ON YEATS'S 'THE WANDERING OF OISIN'

But love is not fashionable any more, the poets have killed it. They wrote so much about it that nobody believed them.

THE REMARKABLE ROCKET

He has always been a great poet. But he has his limitations, the chief of which is, curiously enough, an entire lack of any sense of limit. His song is nearly always too loud for his subject.

ON MR. SWINBURNE'S LAST VOLUME

Every century that produces poetry is, so far, an artificial century, and the work that seems to us to be the most natural and simple product of its time is always the result of the most self-conscious effort.

THE CRITIC AS ARTIST

Anybody can make history. Only a great man can write it.

The Critic as Artist

In Art, the public accept what has been, because they cannot alter it, not because they appreciate it. They swallow their classics whole, and never taste them.

The Soul of Man under Socialism

As for modern journalism, it is not my business to defend it. It justifies its own existence by the great Darwinian principle of the survival of the vulgarest.

The Critic as Artist

I am always amused by the silly vanity of those writers and artists of our day, who seem to imagine that the primary function of the critic is to chatter about their second-rate work.

The Critic as Artist

It was a fatal day when the public discovered that the pen is mightier than the paving-stone, and can be made as offensive as the brickbat.

The Soul of Man under Socialism

I quite admit that modern novels have many good points. All I insist on is that, as a class, they are quite unreadable.

The Decay of Lying

. . . our second-rate litterateurs . . . are the mere body-snatchers of literature. The dust is given to one, and the ashes to another, and the soul is out of their reach.

THE CRITIC AS ARTIST

As one turns over the pages the suspense of the author becomes almost unbearable.

THE DECAY OF LYING

There is much to be said in favour of modern journalism. By giving us the opinions of the uneducated, it keeps us in touch with the ignorance of the community. By carefully chronicling the current events of contemporary life, it shows us what very little importance such events really have.

THE CRITIC AS ARTIST

To have a style so gorgeous that it conceals the subject is one of the highest achievements of an important and much admired school of Fleet Street leader-writers.

The Decay of Lying

The good ended happily, and the bad unhappily. That is what Fiction means.

The Importance of Being Earnest

I dislike modern memoirs. They are generally written by people who have either entirely lost their memories, or have never done anything worth remembering.

The Critic as Artist

Every great man nowadays has his disciples, and it is always Judas who writes the biography.

THE CRITIC AS ARTIST

In fact, the popular novel that the public calls healthy is always a thoroughly unhealthy production; and what the public calls an unhealthy novel is always a beautiful and healthy work of art.

THE SOUL OF MAN UNDER SOCIALISM

The ancient historians gave us delightful fiction in the form of fact; the modern novelist presents us with dull facts under the guise of fiction.

THE CRITIC AS ARTIST

The fact is, that the public have an insatiable curiosity to know everything, except what is worth knowing. Journalism, conscious of this, and having tradesmanlike habits, supplies their demands.

THE SOUL OF MAN UNDER SOCIALISM

In centuries before ours the public nailed the ears of journalists to the pump. That was quite hideous. In this century journalists have nailed their own ears to the keyhole. That is much worse.

THE SOUL OF MAN UNDER SOCIALISM

As for that great and daily increasing school of novelists for whom the sun always rises in the East-End, the only thing that can be said about them is that they find life crude, and leave it raw.

THE DECAY OF LYING

As a rule, the critics – I speak, of course, of the higher class, of those in fact who write for the sixpenny papers – are far more cultured than the people whose work they are called upon to review.

THE CRITIC AS ARTIST

Formerly we used to canonise our heroes. The modern method is to vulgarise them. Cheap editions of great books may be delightful, but cheap editions of great men are absolutely detestable.

THE CRITIC AS ARTIST

Mr. James Payn is an adept in the art of concealing what is not worth finding. He hunts down the obvious with the enthusiasm of a short-sighted detective.

THE DECAY OF LYING

Mr. Marion Crawford has immolated himself upon the altar of local colour. . . he has fallen into a bad habit of uttering moral platitudes. He is always telling us that to be good is to be good, and that to be bad is to be wicked. At times he is almost edifying.

THE DECAY OF LYING

Mr. Henry James writes fiction as if it were a painful duty, and wastes upon mean motives and imperceptible 'points of view' his neat literary style, his felicitous phrases, his swift and caustic satire.

THE DECAY OF LYING

For in some respects Dickens might be likened to those old sculptors of our Gothic cathedrals . . . whose art lacking sanity was therefore incomplete. Yet they at least knew the limitations of their art, while Dickens never knew the limitations of his. When he tries to be serious, he only succeeds in being dull, when he aims at truth, he merely reaches platitude.

A NEW BOOK ON DICKENS

Ah! Meredith! Who can define him? His style is chaos illumined by flashes of lightning. As a writer he has mastered everything except language: as a novelist he can do anything, except tell a story: as an artist he is everything, except articulate.

THE DECAY OF LYING

We fear that Mr. Routledge's edition will not do. It is well printed, and nicely bound; but his translators do not understand French.

ON BALZAC IN ENGLISH

French prose, even in the hands of the most ordinary writers, is always readable, but English prose is unreadable.

English Poetesses

Eloquence is a beautiful thing, but rhetoric ruins many a critic; and Mr. Symonds is essentially rhetorical.

UNSIGNED REVIEW OF MR. SYMONDS' *Life of Ben Jonson*

What right has a man to the title of poet when he fails to produce music in his lines, who cannot express his thoughts in a simple language that the people can understand; but, on the contrary, has so imperfect a command of his mother tongue that all the efforts of a society of intellectual pickaxes cannot discover what his words really mean?

THE POETS AND THE PEOPLE

If Poetry has passed him by, Philosophy will take note of him.

THE GOSPEL ACCORDING TO WALT WHITMAN

With regard to modern journalists, they always apologise to one in private for what they have written against one in public.

THE SOUL OF MAN UNDER SOCIALISM

In modern days . . . the fashion of writing poetry has become far too common, and should, if possible, be discouraged.

THE DECAY OF LYING

Anybody can be reasonable, but to be sane is not common; and sane poets are as rare as blue lilies, though they may not be quite so delightful.

A NOTE ON SOME MODERN POETS [POEMS BY HENLEY AND SHARP]

Old fashions in literature are as pleasant as old fashions in dress. I like the costume of the age of powder better than the poetry of the age of Pope.

English Poetesses

As for the mob, I have no desire to be a popular novelist. It is far too easy.

Defence of Dorian Gray

I am afraid that writing to newspapers has a deteriorating influence on style. People get violent, and abusive, and lose all sense of proportion when they enter that curious journalistic arena in which the race is always to the noisiest.

Defence of Dorian Gray

En Route is most over-rated. It is sheer journalism. It never makes one hear a note of the music it describes. The subject is delightful, but the style is of course worthless, slipshod, flaccid. It is worse French than Ohnet's. Ohnet tries to be commonplace and succeeds. Huysmans tries not to be, and is.

Fourth Letter from Reading Prison

Lady Hunstanton: But do you believe all that is written in the newspapers?

Lord Illingworth: I do. Nowadays it is only the unreadable that occurs.

A Woman of No Importance

The English public like tediousness, and like things to be explained to them in a tedious way.

DEFENCE OF DORIAN GRAY

I am very much pleased to see that you are beginning to call attention to the extremely slipshod and careless style of our ordinary magazine-writers.

HALF HOURS WITH THE WORST AUTHORS

It is proper that limitations should be placed on action. It is not proper that limitations should be placed on art. To art belongs all things that are and things that are not, and even the editor of a London paper has no right to restrain the freedom of art in the selection of subject-matter.

DEFENCE OF DORIAN GRAY

As for the other, the scribblers and nibblers of literature, if they indeed reverence Rossetti's memory, let them pay him the one homage he would most have valued, the gracious homage of silence.

A CHEAP EDITION OF A GREAT MAN

In France, in fact, they limit the journalist and allow the artist almost perfect freedom. Here we allow absolute freedom to the journalist, and entirely limit the artist.

THE SOUL OF MAN UNDER SOCIALISM

How should one stop to listen to the lucubrations of a literary gamin, to the brawling and mouthing of a man whose praise would be as insolent as his slander is impotent, or the irresponsible and irrepressible chatter of the professionally unproductive?

Letter to Joaquin Miller, 28 February 1882

He has no enemies, and none of his friends like him.

ON GEORGE BERNARD SHAW, SEPTEMBER 1886

Let any sensible man outside the Browning Society, dip into the mysterious volume of literary hocus-pocus that has recently been solemnly reviewed, and see whether he can find a single passage likely to stir the pulses of any man or woman, create a desire to lead a higher, a holier, and a more useful life in the breast of the indifferent average citizen.

THE POETS AND THE PEOPLE

There is always something peculiarly impotent about the violence of a literary man.

ON MR. MAHAFFY'S NEW BOOK [*Greek Life and Thought*]

Life by its realism is always spoiling the subject-matter of art.

DEFENCE OF DORIAN GRAY

Lady Hunstanton: I don't know how he made his money, originally.

Kelvil: I fancy in American dry goods.

Lady Hunstanton: What are American dry goods?

Lord Illingworth: American novels.

A WOMAN OF NO IMPORTANCE

The critic has to educate the public; the artist has to educate the critic.

DEFENCE OF DORIAN GRAY

No country produces such badly written fiction, such tedious, common work in the novel-form, such silly, vulgar plays as in England.

THE SOUL OF MAN UNDER SOCIALISM

Algernon: The truth is rarely pure and never simple. Modern life would be very tedious if it were either, and modern literature a complete impossibility!

Jack: That wouldn't be at all a bad thing.

Algernon: Literary criticism is not your forte, my dear fellow. Don't try it. You should leave that to people who haven't been at a University. They do it so well in the daily papers.

THE IMPORTANCE OF BEING EARNEST

You should study the Peerage, Gerald. It is the one book a young man about town should know thoroughly, and it is the best thing in fiction the English have ever done.

A WOMAN OF NO IMPORTANCE

If your pistol is as harmless as your pen, this young tyrant will have a long life.

VERA, OR THE NIHILISTS

I am sure that you must have a great future in literature before you . . . Because you seem to be such a bad interviewer, I feel sure that you must write poetry. I certainly like the colour of your necktie very much.

[INTERVIEW FOR *The Sketch*]

Believe me, sir, Puritanism is never so offensive and destructive as when it deals with art matters.

DEFENCE OF DORIAN GRAY

It is but a sorry task to rip the twisted ravel from the worn garment of a life, and to turn the grout in a drained cup. Better after all that we only know a painter through his vision and a poet through his song, than that the image of a great man should be marred and made mean by the clumsy geniality of good intentions.

A CHEAP EDITION OF A GREAT MAN

As for Rossetti's elaborate system of punctuation, Mr. Knight pays no attention to it whatsoever. Indeed he shows quite a rollicking indifference to all the secrets and subtleties of style, and inserts and removes stops in a manner that is absolutely destructive to the logical beauty of the verse.

A CHEAP EDITION OF A GREAT MAN

Mr. Mahaffy shows an amount of political bias and literary blindness that is quite extraordinary. He might have made his book a work of solid and enduring interest, but he has chosen to give it a merely ephemeral value, and to substitute for the scientific temper of the true historian the prejudice, the flippancy, and the violence of the platform partisan.

ON MR. MAHAFFY'S NEW BOOK [*Green Life and Thought*]

Your critic has cleared himself of the charge of personal malice . . . but he has only done so by a tacit admission that he has really no critical instinct about literature and literary work, which, in one who writes about literature, is, I need hardly say, a much graver fault than malice of any kind.

DEFENCE OF DORIAN GRAY

BLANKETS AND COAL

Since the introduction of printing, and the fatal development of the habit of reading amongst the middle and lower classes of this country, there has been a tendency in literature to appeal more and more to the eye, and less and less to the ear.

THE CRITIC AS ARTIST

I am not at all in favour of amusements for the poor, Jane. Blankets and coal are sufficient.

A WOMAN OF NO IMPORTANCE

If the poor only had profiles there would be no difficulty in solving the problem of poverty.

PHRASES AND PHILOSOPHIES FOR THE USE OF THE YOUNG

There is only one class in the community that thinks more about money than the rich, and that is the poor.

THE SOUL OF MAN UNDER SOCIALISM

It is a sad fact, but there is no doubt that the poor are completely unconscious of their own picturesqueness.

LONDON MODELS

I am glad that she has gone . . . she has a decidedly middle-class mind.

THE REMARKABLE ROCKET

The well-bred contradict other people. The wise contradict themselves.

PHRASES AND PHILOSOPHIES FOR THE USE OF THE YOUNG

Really, if the lower orders don't set us a good example, what on earth is the use of them? They seem, as a class, to have absolutely no sense of moral responsibility.

THE IMPORTANCE OF BEING EARNEST

I quite sympathise with the rage of the English democracy against what they call the vices of the upper orders. The masses feel that drunkenness, stupidity, and immorality should be their own special property and that if anyone of us makes an ass of himself he is poaching on their preserves.

The Picture of Dorian Gray

Lord Goring: Extraordinary thing about the lower classes in England – they are always losing their relations.

Phipps: Yes, my lord! They are extremely fortunate in that respect.

An Ideal Husband

There is always more books than brains in an aristocracy.

Vera, or The Nihilists

'Poor old chap!' said Hughie, 'how miserable he looks! But I suppose to you painters, his face is his fortune?'
'Certainly,' replied Trevor, 'you don't want a beggar to look happy, do you?'

The Model Millionaire

Gardenias and the peerage were his only weaknesses.

The Canterville Ghost

If a man is a gentleman, he knows quite enough, and if he is not a gentleman, whatever he knows is bad for him.

The Picture of Dorian Gray

Lady Basildon: Ah! I hate being educated!

Mrs. Marchmont: So do I. It puts one almost on a level with the commercial classes, doesn't it?

AN IDEAL HUSBAND

'Common sense, indeed!' said the Rocket indignantly; 'you forget that I am very uncommon, and very remarkable.'

THE REMARKABLE ROCKET

The husbands of very beautiful women belong to the criminal classes.

THE PICTURE OF DORIAN GRAY

It is only by not paying one's bills that one can hope to live in the memory of the commercial classes.

PHRASES AND PHILOSOPHIES FOR THE USE OF THE YOUNG

I am sure, Lord Illingworth, you don't think that uneducated people should be allowed to have votes?

A WOMAN OF NO IMPORTANCE

Crime belongs exclusively to the lower orders.

THE PICTURE OF DORIAN GRAY

I know myself that, when I am coming back from the Drawing room, I always feel as if I hadn't a shred on me, except a small shred of decent reputation, just enough to prevent the lower classes making painful observations through the windows of the carriage.

AN IDEAL HUSBAND

The middle classes air their moral prejudices over their gross dinner-tables, and whisper about what they call the profligacies of their betters in order to try and pretend that they are in smart society, and on intimate terms with the people they slander.

THE PICTURE OF DORIAN GRAY

We don't want to be harrowed and disgusted with an account of the doings of the lower orders.

THE DECAY OF LYING

With a proper background women can do anything.

LADY WINDERMERE'S FAN

As for the virtuous poor, one can pity them, of course, but one cannot possibly admire them.

THE SOUL OF MAN UNDER SOCIALISM

All that one should know about modern life is where the Duchesses are; anything else is quite demoralising.

AN IDEAL HUSBAND

Three addresses always inspire confidence, even in tradesmen.

THE IMPORTANCE OF BEING EARNEST

In these modern days to be vulgar, illiterate, common and vicious, seems to give a man a marvellous infinity of rights that his father never dreamed of.

VERA, OR THE NIHILISTS

Cecily: This is no time for wearing the shallow mask of manners. When I see a spade I call it a spade.

Gwendolen: I am glad to say that I have never seen a spade. It is obvious that our social spheres have been widely different.

THE IMPORTANCE OF BEING EARNEST

The Philistine element in life is not the failure to understand Art. Charming people such as fishermen, shepherds, ploughboys, peasants and the like know nothing about Art, and are the very salt of the earth.

DE PROFUNDIS

Ah! How I loathe the Romans! They are rough and common, and they give themselves the airs of noble lords.

SALOMÉ

I saw the governess, Jane . . . She was far too good-looking to be in any respectable household.

A WOMAN OF NO IMPORTANCE

I would much sooner talk scandal in the drawing-room than treason in a cellar. Besides, I hate the common mob, who smell of garlic, smoke bad tobacco, get up early, and dine off one dish.

VERA, OR THE NIHILISTS

What is our son at present? An underpaid clerk in a small Provincial Bank in a third-rate English town.

A WOMAN OF NO IMPORTANCE

The Cantervilles have blue blood, for instance, the very bluest in England; but I know you Americans don't care for things of this kind.

THE CANTERVILLE GHOST

I don't think that Lord Crediton cared very much for Cyril. He had never forgiven his daughter for marrying a man who had no title. He was an extraordinary old aristocrat, who swore like a costermonger, and had the manners of a farmer.

THE PORTRAIT OF MR. W.H.

The English aristocracy supply us with our curiosities, Lady Caroline. They are sent over to us every summer, regularly, in the steamers, and propose to us the day after they land.

A WOMAN OF NO IMPORTANCE

The world is simply divided into two classes – those who believe the incredible, like the public – and those who do the improbable.

A WOMAN OF NO IMPORTANCE

But birds and lizards have no sense of repose, and indeed birds have not even a permanent address. They are mere vagrants like the gypsies, and should be treated in exactly the same manner.

THE BIRTHDAY OF THE INFANTA

The impulse of the Irish literature of their time came from a class that did not – mainly for political reasons – take the populace seriously, and imagined the country as a humorist's Arcadia . . . What they did was not wholly false, they merely magnified an irresponsible type, found oftenest among boatmen, carmen, and gentlemen's servants, into the type of a whole nation, and created the stage-Irishman.

YEATS'S FAIRY AND FOLK TALES

Believe me, Prince, in a good democracy, every man should be an aristocrat: but these people in Russia who seek to thrust us out are no better than the animals in one's preserves, and made to be shot at, most of them.

VERA, OR THE NIHILISTS

To be born, or at any rate bred, in a hand-bag, whether it had handles or not, seems to me to display a contempt for the ordinary decencies of family life that reminds one of the worst excesses of the French Revolution.

THE IMPORTANCE OF BEING EARNEST

Lady Hunstanton: I hear you have such pleasant society in America. Quite like our own in places, my son wrote to me.

Hester: There are cliques in America as elsewhere, Lady Hunstanton. But true American society consists simply of all the good women and good men we have in our country.

Lady Hunstanton: What a sensible system, and I dare say quite pleasant, too. I am afraid in England we have too many artificial social barriers. We don't see as much as we should of the middle and lower classes.

A WOMAN OF NO IMPORTANCE

Half-past six! What an hour! It will be like having a meat-tea, or reading an English novel. It must be seven. No gentleman dines before seven.

THE PICTURE OF DORIAN GRAY

There are the poor, and amongst them there is no grace of manner, or charm of speech, or civilisation, or culture, or refinement in pleasures, or joy of life.

THE SOUL OF MAN UNDER SOCIALISM

When Jesus talks about the poor he simply means personalities, just as when he talks about the rich he simply means people who have not developed their personalities.

THE SOUL OF MAN UNDER SOCIALISM

To be good, according to the vulgar standard of goodness, is obviously quite easy. It merely requires a certain amount of sordid terror, a certain lack of imaginative thought, and a certain low passion for middle-class respectability.

THE ARTIST AS CRITIC

SIN AND CYNICISM

I am sure the Clergyman himself could not say such beautiful things as you do, though he does live in a three-storied house, and wear a gold ring on his little finger.

THE DEVOTED FRIEND

To die for one's theological beliefs is the worst use a man can make of his life.

The Portrait of Mr. W.H.

'Religion?'
'The fashionable substitute for Belief.'

The Picture of Dorian Gray

Look at the successful men in any of the professions. How perfectly hideous they are! Except, of course, in the Church. But then in the Church they don't think. A bishop keeps on saying at the age of eighty what he was told to say when he was a boy of eighteen, and as a natural consequence he always looks absolutely delightful.

The Picture of Dorian Gray

It is the confession, not the priest that gives us absolution.

The Picture of Dorian Gray

Cecil Graham: What is a cynic?

Lord Darlington: A man who knows the price of everything and the value of nothing.

Lady Windermere's Fan

They love me very much – simple, loyal people; give them a new saint, it costs nothing.

Vera, or The Nihilists

Religions die when they are proved to be true. Science is the record of dead religions.

PHRASES AND PHILOSOPHIES FOR THE USE OF THE YOUNG

Sir Robert Chiltern: But may I ask, at heart, are you an optimist or a pessimist? Those seem to be the only two fashionable religions left to us nowadays.

Mrs. Cheveley: Oh, I'm neither. Optimism begins in a broad grin, and Pessimism ends with blue spectacles.

AN IDEAL HUSBAND

Shallow speakers and shallow thinkers in pulpits and on platforms often talk about the world's worship of pleasure, and whine against it.

THE SOUL OF MAN UNDER SOCIALISM

In the English Church a man succeeds, not through his capacity for belief, but through his capacity for disbelief. Ours is the only Church where the sceptic stands at the altar, and where St. Thomas is regarded as the ideal apostle.

THE DECAY OF LYING

To the wickedness of the Papacy humanity owes much. The goodness of the Papacy owes a terrible debt to humanity.

THE SOUL OF MAN UNDER SOCIALISM

Nothing makes one so vain as being told that one is a sinner.

THE PICTURE OF DORIAN GRAY

Even a colour-sense is more important, in the development of the individual, than a sense of right and wrong.

THE CRITIC AS ARTIST

In matters of grave importance, style, not sincerity, is the vital thing.

THE IMPORTANCE OF BEING EARNEST

The basis of every scandal is an absolutely immoral certainty.

A WOMAN OF NO IMPORTANCE

Lady Stutfield: There is nothing, nothing like the beauty of home-life, is there?

Kelvil: It is the mainstay of our moral system in England, Lady Stutfield. Without it we would become like our neighbours.

A WOMAN OF NO IMPORTANCE

Wickedness is a myth invented by good people to account for the curious attractiveness of others.

PHRASES AND PHILOSOPHIES FOR THE USE OF THE YOUNG

All crime is vulgar, just as vulgarity is crime.

THE PICTURE OF DORIAN GRAY

My dear Rachel, intellectual generalities are always interesting, but generalities in morals mean absolutely nothing.

A Woman of No Importance

Conscience and cowardice are really the same things . . . Conscience is the trade name of the firm. That is all.

The Picture of Dorian Gray

Conscience is but the name which cowardice
Fleeing from battle scrawls upon its shield.

The Duchess of Padua

Charity, as even those of whose religion it makes a formal part have been compelled to acknowledge, creates a multitude of evils.

The Critic as Artist

A man who moralises is usually a hyprocrite, and a woman who moralises is invariably plain.

Lady Windermere's Fan

A little sincerity is a dangerous thing, and a great deal of it is absolutely fatal.

The Critic as Artist

There is nothing in the whole world so unbecoming to a woman as a Nonconformist conscience.

Lady Windermere's Fan

Sentimentality is merely the Bank Holiday of cynicism.

De Profundis

What people call insincerity is simply a method by which we can multiply our personalities.

The Critic as Artist

The only difference between the saint and the sinner is that every saint has a past, and every sinner has a future.

A Woman of No Importance

I can't understand this modern mania for curates. In my time we girls saw them, of course, running about the place like rabbits. But we never took any notice of them, I need hardly say. But I am told that nowadays country society is quite honeycombed with them. I think it most irreligious.

An Ideal Husband

'How well you talk!' said the Miller's Wife, pouring herself out a large glass of warm ale; 'really I feel quite drowsy. It is just like being in church.'

The Devoted Friend

It is very difficult to keep awake, especially at church.

The Canterville Ghost

Experience is the name everyone gives to their mistakes.

Lady Windermere's Fan

Man can believe the impossible, but man can never believe the improbable.

THE DECAY OF LYING

As for the Church, I cannot conceive anything better for the culture of a country than the presence in it of a body of men whose duty it is to believe in the supernatural, to perform miracles, and to keep alive that mythopoeic faculty which is so essential for the imagination.

THE DECAY OF LYING

A wet Sunday, an uncouth Christian in a mackintosh, a ring of sickly white faces under a broken roof of umbrellas, and wonderful phrase flung into the air by shrill, hysterical lips . . .

THE PICTURE OF DORIAN GRAY

The things one feels absolutely certain about are never true. That is the fatality of Faith, and the lesson of Romance.

THE PICTURE OF DORIAN GRAY

One can survive everything nowadays, except death, and live down anything except a good reputation.

A WOMAN OF NO IMPORTANCE

The two weak points in our age are its want of principle and its want of profile.

THE IMPORTANCE OF BEING EARNEST

The costume of the nineteenth century is detestable. It is so sombre, so depressing. Sin is the only real colour-element left in modern life.

THE PICTURE OF DORIAN GRAY

All repetition is anti-spiritual.

DE PROFUNDIS

Modern morality consists in accepting the standard of one's age. I consider that for any man of culture to accept the standard of his age is a form of the grossest immorality.

THE PICTURE OF DORIAN GRAY

And there was also, I remember, a clergyman who wanted to be a lunatic, or a lunatic who wanted to be a clergyman, I forget which . . .

A WOMAN OF NO IMPORTANCE

The man who sees both sides of a question, is a man who sees absolutely nothing at all.

THE CRITIC AS ARTIST

It is only the shallow people who require years to get rid of an emotion.

THE PICTURE OF DORIAN GRAY

Secrets from other people's wives are a necessary luxury in modern life. So, at least, I am always told at the club by people who are bald enough to know better.

AN IDEAL HUSBAND

What is termed Sin is an essential element of progress. Without it the world would stagnate, or grow old, or become colourless.

THE CRITIC AS ARTIST

Manners before morals!

LADY WINDERMERE'S FAN

Those who see any difference between soul and body have neither.

PHRASES AND PHILOSOPHIES FOR THE USE OF THE YOUNG

The only thing that sustains one through life is the consciousness of the immense inferiority of everybody else, and this is a feeling I have always cultivated.

THE REMARKABLE ROCKET

Murder is always a mistake . . . One should never do anything that one cannot talk about after dinner.

THE PICTURE OF DORIAN GRAY

To morals belong the lower and less intellectual spheres.

THE CRITIC AS ARTIST

Early in life she had discovered the important truth that nothing looks so like innocence as an indiscretion; and by a series of escapades, half of them quite harmless, she had acquired all the privileges of a personality.

LORD ARTHUR SAVILE'S CRIME

Dullness is the coming of age of seriousness.

PHRASES AND PHILOSOPHIES FOR THE USE OF THE YOUNG

What a Communist the Prince is! He would have an equal distribution of sin as well as of property.

VERA, OR THE NIHILISTS

If one tells the truth, one is sure, sooner or later, to be found out.

PHRASES AND PHILOSOPHIES FOR THE USE OF THE YOUNG

In fact, you should be thinking about me. I am always thinking about myself, and I expect everybody else to do the same. That is what is called sympathy. It is a beautiful virtue, and I possess it in a high degree.

THE REMARKABLE ROCKET

Morality is simply the attitude we adopt towards people whom we personally dislike.

An Ideal Husband

Good resolutions are useless attempts to interfere with scientific laws. Their origin is pure vanity. Their result is absolutely nil. They give us, now and then, some of those luxurious emotions that have a certain charm for the weak.

The Picture of Dorian Gray

We cannot go back to the saint. There is far more to be learned from the sinner.

The Critic as Artist

Ideals are dangerous things. Realities are better.

Lady Windermere's Fan

There is no such thing as a moral or an immoral book. Books are well written, or badly written. That is all.

The Picture of Dorian Gray

What a mistake it is to be sincere!

Vera, or The Nihilists

It is always a silly thing to give advice, but to give good advice is absolutely fatal.

THE PORTRAIT OF MR. W.H.

They were stupid enough to have principles, and unfortunate enough to act up to them.

ON 'A CHINESE SAGE' [CONFUCIUS]

All excess, as well as all renunciation, brings its own punishment.

DEFENCE OF DORIAN GRAY

Those who find ugly meanings in beautiful things are corrupt without being charming.

THE PICTURE OF DORIAN GRAY

They all come to bad ends, and showed that universal altruism is as bad in its results as universal egotism.

ON 'A CHINESE SAGE' [CONFUCIUS]

Oh, I hate the cheap severity of abstract ethics.

THE CANTERVILLE GHOST

There are few things easier than to live badly and to die well.

VERA, OR THE NIHILISTS

I did not sell myself for money. I bought success at a great price.

AN IDEAL HUSBAND

Ah! It is so easy to convert others. It is so difficult to convert oneself.

The Critic as Artist

For what is Truth? In matters of religion, it is simply the opinion that has survived.

The Decay of Lying

When people agree with me I always feel that I must be wrong.

The Critic as Artist

One should never take sides in anything. . . Taking sides is the beginning of sincerity, and earnestness follows shortly afterwards, and the human being becomes a bore.

A Woman of No Importance

There is a fatality about all good resolutions. They are invariably made too soon.

Phrases and Philosophies for the Use of the Young

There is no essential incongruity between crime and culture. We cannot re-write the whole of history for the purpose of gratifying our moral sense of what should be.

The Critic as Artist

Indifference is the revenge the world takes on mediocrities.

Vera, or The Nihilists

Sins of the flesh are nothing. They are maladies for physicians to cure, if they should be cured. Sins of the soul alone are shameful.

De Profundis

As long as war is regarded as wicked, it will always have its fascination.

THE CRITIC AS ARTIST

Crime in England is rarely the result of sin. It is nearly always the result of starvation.

THE CRITIC AS ARTIST

A truth ceases to be true when more than one person believes in it.

PHRASES AND PHILOSOPHIES FOR THE USE OF THE YOUNG

Any preoccupation with ideas of what is right or wrong in conduct shows an arrested intellectual development.

PHRASES AND PHILOSOPHIES FOR THE USE OF THE YOUNG

Indiscretion is the better part of valour.

THE CRITIC AS ARTIST

An idea that is not dangerous is unworthy of being called an idea at all.

THE CRITIC AS ARTIST

Man is least himself when he talks in his own person. Give him a mask, and he will tell you the truth.

THE CRITIC AS ARTIST

The world is a stage, but the play is badly cast.

LORD ARTHUR SAVILE'S CRIME

The only horrible thing in the world is ennui . . . That is the one sin for which there is no forgiveness.

THE PICTURE OF DORIAN GRAY

Life is simply a *mauvais quart d'heure* made up of exquisite moments.

A WOMAN OF NO IMPORTANCE

When the gods wish to punish us they answer our prayers.

AN IDEAL HUSBAND

In the soul of one who is ignorant there is always room for a great idea.

DE PROFUNDIS

We are all in the gutter, but some of us are looking at the stars.

LADY WINDERMERE'S FAN